The MYSTERY *of* HUMAN SUFFERING

The
MYSTERY
of HUMAN
SUFFERING

JOSEPH FITZPATRICK OYONE MEYE

XULON PRESS

Xulon Press
2301 Lucien Way #415
Maitland, FL 32751
407.339.4217
www.xulonpress.com

Unless otherwise indicated, Scripture quotations taken from the King James Version (KJV)–public domain.

Printed in the United States of America.

ISBN-13: 978-1-6312-9029-9

Table of Contents

PART THREE
SIN & INIQUITY

PART FOUR
POLITICS

PART FIVE
SPIRITUAL PRINCIPLES

PART SIX
THE ABSENCE OF LOVE IS THE PRESENCE OF EVIL

PART SEVEN
THE PASSION OF THE CHRIST

PART EIGHT
THE PARTICIPATION IN THE PASSION OF THE CHRIST

FINAL WORDS

Man who is born of a woman is few of days and full of trouble,
like a flower that springs up and withers, swift as a shadow that
does not abides.

JOB 14:1-2

INTRODUCTION

WHY DOES A LOVING GOD ALLOW SUFFERING?

Why Does a Loving God Allow Suffering?

The predicted suffering of mankind is one of the major aspects of biblical prophecy concerning the future of the earth. It is paradoxical that Man chosen for exaltation and selected to be a special means of divine revelation should also be destined for suffering.

GOD is infinitely good and all his works are good. Yet no one can escape the experience of suffering or the evils in nature which seem to be linked to the limitations proper to creatures: and above all to the questions of moral evils. We all know what it is to feel pain and loss. Whether from the loss of a loved one, a sickness, a disease, an infirmity in your body, or a natural disaster, everyone experiences suffering. Suffering isn't an elective course, it's not optional. Even if a person owns a private jet, an island, lives in a mansion and has a great job with loaded bank accounts, suffering touches everybody and affects everybody's faith.

For years I have wondered why does a loving God allow suffering? This age-old question is especially predominant during times of great strife, suffering and despair. If God is all knowing, all powerful, kind, loving and merciful, how is it that He allows suffering to come in your life and my life with seemingly insurmountable, even devastating situations? This is one of the most important questions of human history and yet it exists like an open wound that can never be cure. This question is the basis of what is known as "theodicy" or the rational attempt to explain how God can be omnipotent and all-good and yet allow suffering and evil to exist.

Let me tell you, God hate suffering. He does not take pleasure in our sufferings; He does not rejoice over our sufferings, He did not created us and make this world and intended us to suffer. Not at all. God is not responsible to all of the bad things that is going on in your life and my life or in the earth or in this world. God is not. God is not the author of suffering and of the sufferings of this world, and this is where we are mistaken and questioning the goodness of God. Here are three points that we need to understand.

The first point that we must understand is that there is a mechanism of warning and judgment set up against mankind and the earth in the heavenly place, it's like a time bomb, something with a potentially dangerous or detrimental delayed reaction, a bomb so made as to explode at a predetermined time and that time is when man refused to obeyed God's laws, spiritual principles and God's commandments, or when Nations refused to listen to Him and His way, when sin reached a certain proportion and sin reached its full measure, that mechanism takes effect right away and God's judgment sets in, and pain, natural disaster take place.

Job 1:6-12. There was a day when the sons of God came to present themselves before the LORD, and Satan also came among them. And the LORD said to Satan, "From where have you come?" Then Satan answered the LORD and said, "From roaming the earth, going to and fro from it, and from walking up and down on it and patrolling it." And the LORD said to Satan, "Have you noticed and considered my servant Job, and that there is no one on earth like him, blameless and upright, who fears God and turns away avoiding evil?" but Satan answered the Lord and said, Does Job fear God for no reason? Have you not surrounded him and his family and all that he has with your protection? "You have blessed the work of his hands, and his livestock are spread over the land. But now put forth your hand and touch anything that he has, and surely he will blaspheme you and curse you to your face." And the LORD said to Satan, "Behold, all that he has is in your power; only do not lay a hand upon his person." So Satan went out from the presence of the LORD. The story goes with Job facing Suffering, God allowed Satan to test Job. Satan went forth from the presence of the Lord and Job faced many trials, Satan took Job's property and children and he went on to attack Job's health. (Job 1-2-3). Satan is the author of suffering, and what God does is, He permit, God allows Satan to test us, He allows Satan to tempt us, he allows Satan to attack us, and to try us, to bring calamities and disasters in our lives that's the second point.

The third point God is not a dictator; He is not a ruler with total power over you and me although He is God omnipotent and creator of all things. He did not create us (Man) as robot. God loves us so much that He gave each and every one of us the gift of free will. This free will means that while we are free to do good, we also have the ability to do evil. God chose to give men free will so that we could journey freely to our ultimate destiny. Besides making good choices that bring greater love into the world, we can also make sinful choices that bring evil into the world. God does not in any way cause moral evil, but He respects our freedom by allowing us to choose it. For instance, on the morning of Tuesday, September 11th, 2001. A series of four coordinated terrorist attack by Al Qaeda against the United States. The attacks killed more than 3000 people, injured over 6000 others, and caused more than $ 10 billion in infrastructure and property damage. Additional people died of 9/11, related cancer and respiratory diseases in the months and years following the attacks. Four passenger airliners operated by two major U.S. passenger air carriers (United Airlines and American Airlines) all of which departed from Airport in the northeastern United States bound for California were hijacked by 19 Al-Qaeda terrorists. Two of the planes, American Airlines Flight II and United Flight 175, were crashed into the North and South Towers, respectively, of the World Trade Center complex in lower Manhattan in New York City. Within an hour and 42 minutes, both 110 story towers collapsed. Debris and the resulting fires caused a partial or complete collapse of all other buildings in the World Trade Center Complex, including 47- story 7 World Trade center tower, as well as significant damage to ten other large surrounding structures. A third plane, American Airlines Flight 77, was crashed into the Pentagon (Headquarters of the U.S Department of Defense) in Arlington county, Virginia, which led to a partial collapse of the buildings west side. The fourth plane, United Airline Flight 93, was initially flown toward Washington D.C., but crashed into a fled in Stonycreek Township near Shanks Ville, Pennsylvania, after its passengers thwarted the hijackers. 9/11 is the single deadliest terrorist attack in human history and the single deadliest incident for firefighters and law enforcement officers in the history of the United States, with 343 and 72 killed, respectively. This tragedy certainly brought this question to the minds of many people and many families' victims of this terrorist attack. If God really loves us, why does He permit this terrorism to occur? While the brutally honest and truthful answer is that "He's God and he knows every-thing." The Islamic terrorist group who caused the September 11th attacks in New York chose to commit an evil act. In no way did God cause this to happen.

Free will; Gift of GOD

Certain assumptions about the nature of our freedom usually lurk behind this question. Most people in the West including Christians unconsciously accept what is usually called the "Libertarian view" of free will. This understanding of human freedom says that we have the ability to make spontaneous choices contrary to our dispositions and inclinations. Nothing determines our choices. We are always able to choose good or evil. Our wills are wholly neutral.

Human beings always choose according to their disposition and their strongest desire, and so we make free choices. We do what we want to do. Some may object that people often choose the undesirable, such as handing a purse or a wallet over a mugger. But even if I do this, my strongest inclination has prompted my choice. All things being equal, I do not desire to give my purse or my wallet away. But if my choice is my purse or my wallet or my life, and I hand over my wallet, I prove that I want to live more than I want money.

Free will gives us the ability to make decisions, we are able to decide which clothes we will wear, which school to attend or which profession to exercise. Therefore, good God from on High gave us a gift call free will, the ability to make choices. God purpose with mankind is to have eternal fellowship with those who truly love Him. Therefore, to create us as inherently good robots, without the potential for the opposite character, evil, would not allow for true love. And God is so good that His gifts are irrevocable. For instance, He sent Jesus Christ His only Son who gave His life for the sin of the world and thus offer Eternal life, He does not even force us to accept the Gospel, He does not impose us to receive Jesus Christ as Lord and Savior. But if you decide to accept the Gospel and receive Jesus in your life, God will bless you and teach you how to use your free will and to become like Christ. Free will is an eternal law that has always existed from all eternity, and will continue to exist in all eternity to come. To use free will, we must have choices to make, if we are able to make choices, but there is no choice, we do not have free will. In other words, we can only choose if there is a choice to make. The main use of our free will is to choose between good and evil, life or death. Satan' purpose is to fight good, his purpose is to fight righteousness, his purpose is to fight love. But if we don't yield to Satan' temptation and decide to obey God and the law of good then the world would be a better place to live in.

The Lord knew that in our choices we would be influenced by good and evil. Without this conflict between good and evil, we would have no choice; we would have no free will. The Lord therefore gives us principles, laws and commandment to obey and Satan pushes us, influences us to disobey and break them. Apart from Christ, we are dead in sin and wholly disposed to hate God. We only want darkness (St John 3:19), and so we freely choose to reject Him. We freely choose to love and serve God in Jesus only if the Spirit changes our heart. Otherwise we remain lost.

Part One

ORIGIN OF EVIL & THE CAUSE OF HUMAN SUFFERING

You became haughty of heart because of your beauty; you corrupted your wisdom for the sake of your splendor, I cast you to the earth, so great was your guilt.

Ezekiel 27:17-18

The Angelical Sphere

I'd like to start this topic by sharing with you some spiritual principles and impart you some spiritual knowledge to understand. The first thing that you must understand is that, this life, the life that we are in, this world is first and foremost spiritual. In other words, this life is governed by the spiritual. Therefore, there is what we called spiritual laws, also known as laws of the spirits. And just as the laws of nature exist, the spiritual laws exist as well as the physical laws. The spiritual laws dominate on the law of nature and dominate on the physical laws. Those laws governed us and governed this world. And whether you are aware or not, these laws exist and governed the world of mankind and the universe. Everything that is spiritual governs anything that is physical. Spiritual laws can acts in our lives positively if we practices them or negatively or against us if we ignored them or if we don't practice them. This life is first and foremost spiritual. Job 32:8 says, "But it is a spirit in man." In other words, this body of flesh, this envelop was given to us to live in this world, but everything in us work according to the spirit in us. Life is first and foremost spiritual.

After having created the Heavens and the Earth, GOD creates spiritual beings, angels, who are ministering spirits to serves him. God was sitting on his throne and the stars of the morning (angels) were singing worshiping, praising and were glorifying God. The Lord spread them out into different groups called Angelical Spheres. They are 12 angelic celestial orders or hierarchy, and each angelic order has its special purpose for existing: and divided in 4 choirs:

3

The First Choir:

- The Supernals Well known (Michael)
- The Celestials Well known (Astarael)
- The Illuminations Well known (Sandalphon)

The Second Choir:

- The Seraphims Well known (Michael, Metatron)
- The Cherubims Well known (Lucifer before his fall, Cherubiel, Gabriel)
- The Thrones or Ophanim Well known (Bodiel, Jophiel, Zaphkiel, Oriphiel, Raziel)

The Third Choir:

- The Dominations or Lordships Well known (Hashmal, Zadkiel, Muriel, Zacharael)
- The Virtues or Stronghold Well known (Chamuel, Uriel, Gabriel, Michael),
- The Powers or Authority Well known (Gabriel, Raphael, Verchiel)

The Fourth Choir:

- The Principalities or Rulers Well known (Anael, Haniel, Cerviel, Amael,, Requel)
- The Archangels Well known (Gabriel, Raphael, Michael, Metatron, Uriel)
- The Angels Well known (Gabriel, Raphael, Chayyliel, Phaleg, Adnachiel)

Each order has its special purpose for existing.

Among those myriads and myriads of angels, God chose one, he was very beautiful, light was shining all over his body, his body was shining light like precious jewels, jasper and God gave him many privileges and gave him a specific mission which was to worship God, it was that cherubim angel who gave God the worship songs, the music, the hymns. His other mission was also to transmit light to the entire angelical sphere. And since his mission was to transmit light, God gave that angel a name and the name was Lucifer.

God's purpose for His angelic creation was derailed the moment Lucifer turned against God's law to the way of lawlessness and rebellion. Why should there be so much ignorance about Lucifer the devil? Many people scoff at the thought of his existence. Others, while they accept his existence, grossly underestimate the devil's power. They assume that his deceptive influence over the world is limited and easy to detect. On the other hand, there are those who think God and Satan are engaged in a tug-of-war over the "souls" of men. In this scenario-judging by the sheer number of people who have lived and died without ever having accepted Jesus as their Savior-Satan is clearly depicted as being stronger than God. The reason for this ignorance is because Satan, as the god of this world, has blinded the minds of men from the truth about his existence, his rule on earth and his fate in God's master plan.

Lucifer; the Prince of Darkness

Lucifer is a Latin word and when you divided that name in two, the first is Luci (light) the second is fer (carrier) Lucifer, carrier of light or angel of light. His face was looking non stop at the one who was sitting on the throne namely God.

Ezekiel 28:12-17, And God says: You were anointed guardian cherubim; you were stamped with the seal of perfection, of complete wisdom and perfect beauty. In Eden, the garden of God,

5

you were, and every precious stone was your covering (carnelian, topaz, and beryl, chrysolite, onyx, and jasper, sapphire, garnet, and emerald); of gold your pendant and jewels were made, on the day you were created. With the Cherubim I placed you; you were on the holy mountain of God, walking among the fiery stones. Blameless you were in your conduct from the day you were created, until evil was found in you, the result of your far-flung trade; you were filled with violence in your midst and you sinned. Then I banned you as a profane thing from the mountain of God, and I destroyed you, the Cherub drove you from among the fiery stones. You became haughty of heart because of your beauty; you corrupted your wisdom for the sake of your splendor, I cast you to the earth, so great was your guilt (Ezekiel 28:12-17).

Lucifer's Rebellion: War in Heaven:

Lucifer after a while stopped looking at God and began to look at his beauty and his abilities (That's how pride begin, whenever we begin to look at ourselves and talk about ourselves, Me, Me Me, I, I, I and we stop talking about God and stop looking at God but ourselves, it's the beginning of pride), Lucifer became prideful and he coveted the throne of God, he wanted God's place and was committed to dethroned God in order to take the place of the Creator and so that every one (angels) in the heavenly place will worshiped him instead. Lucifer began to conspire against God he wanted the angels to look at him and thus stop looking at God the Creator. And to accomplished and fulfill his desires Lucifer began to deceived his fellow angels and start plotting all kind of things and ended up corrupting the heart of his companions the others angels of God. Lucifer corrupted 1/3 of the angels and made his team. With those he formed an army called The Mystery of the Air (Member of the Lucifer' Government) that's the reason the Bible called him in the book of (Ephesians 2:2) the prince of the power of the air. With that army, they declared war in Heaven to fight against the other angels who remain faithful to God (Rev 12:7). Michael and his angels fought against them and the dragon (Lucifer) and his angels fought back, but Lucifer was defeated and realized that he wasn't that strong. This rebellion against established order brought divine judgment and Lucifer, with a great number of angelic beings who followed him, was judged in a titanic fall. Lucifer's name was changed to Satan, and from his arrogance was born an unending hatred of God.

After the defeat of Satan, there was no longer any place in heaven for them and thus Lucifer was cast to the earth and his angels were thrown down with him

And the Bible says therefore rejoice O heavens, and you who dwell in them! Woe to the inhabitants of the earth and the sea! For the devil has come down to you having great wrath because he knows that he has a short time. (Rev 12:8-12)

Woe to you, Earth & Sea, for Satan has come down to you in Great Fury

Earth is 50% cover with water, waters take more place then the earth itself, and by deduction we can conclude that there was many fallen angels on the waters (sea) than on the earth. Therefore there are fallen angels on earth and also in the sea, and the prophet Ezekiel 28:18 says: Because of your guilt, your sinful trade, the multitude of your covenants, in other words when the devil was thrown down, he made covenants with those fallen angels that followed him. They came down to earth, and since he didn't have what he was looking for in heaven, he decided that he was going to have it on earth. Lucifer wants power, he wants praise unto him, he wants worship unto him, he want to be glorified, and he wants to be exalted. Lucifer Satan shared his power with some of the fallen angels and made covenants with them and took territories

7

on the face of the earth to ruled and reign. Some in fallen angels or demons went to the mountains and rule there, some went to the seas and rule there, some went to the rivers and rule there, some went to the hills and reign there and other went to the forests and reign there. Jesus Christ called Lucifer, the prince of this world, in other word, he is the one who controlled the world, and established some of the fallen angels, powerful and established them in territories in the earth.

The devil coming down on earth has always trying to send God a message by telling him that if I (Satan) missed the worship and praise in heaven, I'm going to have it here on earth, me and my territorial spirits, in each country, each culture, each village, and I will conquer the heart of man and will give them spiritual belief so that they will believe in me and worship me. That's why you see in every nation and people, each one called god in his own way. Now who are they? It's not the God of Israel, the Creator but those territorial spirits that seduced man to worship them, so that what the devil has missed in heaven, he can have it here on earth. In the book of Ephesians some are called principalities. And on each nation of the earth, there are principalities established, spirits ruling in a specific area, territory, for instance the one who is reigning here in the USA is not the same who is reigning in France and so forth. Each territory has a particular spirit and they are called principalities. And whenever we talked about principalities, we talked about principles and those spirits reigning in territory, it is they that had infiltrated the territory, the country, the village, the society by imparting them principles that are often against the word of God, and the people mentality and culture are coming from those spirits, they had been influenced by those spirits, that's why a Christian does not have any other culture or mentality than the culture and mentality of the Kingdom of Christ.

In the course of Lucifer's rebellion, he attempted to raise his earthly throne-yes, Lucifer has a throne, but God, in a literal sense, brought Lucifer back down to earth. He changed his name to Satan, which means adversary. And the angels who rebelled with Lucifer became demons. In all this, however, God did not remove Satan from the throne of this earth. This is why, when Satan offered Jesus Christ "all the kingdoms of the world" in St Matthew 4, Jesus did not deny that Satan was now ruling over the nations of men.

Lucifer' Chosen People

Many people think that the devil is on the earth and in the seas, but the devil is in the air, precisely in the second heaven. When we look up, the sky that we're seeing is the first heaven where the birds and the airplanes fly, after that one come the second heaven where the sun, moon and the stars are, then the third Heaven, the Heaven of God, God's dwelling place.

Lucifer fell in the second heaven and he created a world called The World of Tartarus. The second heaven is a place where the devil reign with the fallen angels (144,000) and they are in the air. Satan did not come to the earth although he has access to it, but he does not live on earth or under the earth or under the sea. Satan stays in the airs, he err in the airs in the second heaven in a place called the world of Tartarus. It is from the second heaven that the devil and his fallen angels look down to the earth and watch carefully and studied the entire human race and came with a conclusion. After having seriously studied mankind, Satan concluded that there are 3 categories of people:

1. The first category of mankind is people having hatred and jealousy within themselves from the past experience and are looking and seeking to destroy at no cost and for no gain. These kinds of people the Satan gave them the color black.
2. The second category of mankind that Satan likes are people able to kill, shed innocent or guilty blood for the glory of

this world (money, power, domination, fame, glory). To them the Satan gave the color red.

3. The third category is people looking and seeking to know the why of everything, and seek to explain the existence of God through science. To them the devil gave the color white.

It is from these three colors that the existence of the three bad ones came, namely the three magic (the black magic, the red magic and the white magic).

These three magic are connected to each other's by a code resuming the power of the mystery of the air. The Black Magic is very spread throughout the world and is practiced throughout the earth under the sun with those who are alive consulting the world of the dead. Those people who are dead in evil and did not repent from their evil deeds. Demons generally are behind those ancestors. It's not truly those ancestors who are coming to answer but demons who take the form and the voice of those ancestors to deceive the living who consult them. The black magic is divided in many branches and one of its branches is WICHCRAFT. The Red Magic is practice on the earth under the sun for the purpose of riches, power, domination and fame, in other word the glory of this world through victim (Sacrifice killing, rituals killing...) Red is an adjective qualifying blood. The White Magic is divided in many branches, and they are OCCULTS SCIENCE, Secret Society. This is the origin of evil and how Satan set it up.

Lucifer' Enemies

Satan has three types of enemies. The first type is the woman. Why? Because she gave birth to a child (Jesus) who came to destroy the works of the devil. It is also the woman who keeps on giving birth to children (servants of God) who are destroying the works of the devil. The second category is whosoever who keep God's commandments and keep the testimony of Jesus Christ, and any man who gave is life to Jesus became automatically Satan/ enemy. The third type is whosoever born of a woman, including them who work for Satan as the witches, the warlocks, the wizards. For Satan they are all enemies although they work for him but it doesn't matter to him and they will found it out only when they are dead.

The Church the Body of Christ is the visible part of the army of Jesus Christ and the angels are the invisible part of the army of Jesus. Satan came up with key actions plan to come against mankind especially the church of Jesus Christ. Here are few actions plan:

- Fight and Oppose the manifestation of the Holy Spirit
- Enforce the power of evil and overcome evil with evil
- Introduction of homosexuality, Lesbianism and Gay marriages
- Twist and distort the Bible
- Corrupt Almighty God's servants and Deceive His people
- Promote Hatred, Jalousie, Sadism, Disrespect and Destruction in the church and the world

Here are the Ten Commandments of Lucifer:

The Ten Commandments of Lucifer

1. Do not allows Christians to pray and to fast (create heaviness on them)
2. Do not allows Christians to read the Bible (keep them ignorant)
3. Harden Christians heart not to pay the tithe and the offerings, and tell them that God does not need them but that pastors steal them
4. Keep at all cost the Christians poor
5. Spread hatred throughout the world especially among the Christians and between Christian and divided churches

6. Not allows Christians to teach, testify and preach the Glory of God
7. Spread polygamy in churches and thus gives souls to the devil
8. Submit Christians to worship images and idols
9. 2fold Commandments: A- Submit to Christians the tradition of the elders and the worship of dead (ancestors). B- Submit Christian to watch tv and thus could not resist to temptation
10. Do not pronounce the Name of God the Creator and His only Son Jesus Christ.

Lucifer' Ministry

When we talk about Lucifer's ministry and his demons, we must also understand that Satan has 6 ministers and he himself makes seven. As we know that one week is made out of seven days. Satan has assigned a demon every day of our lives to a specific mission. Know also that demons work 24h. This is how Satan and his demons operate every day Monday to Sunday.

On Monday: Satan himself work as a minister and his mission is to destroy in all areas of life (John 10:10). If you pay close attention, Monday is a day where things don't always work well and we feel heavy. On Tuesday: A minister of Satan, a demon work and his mission is to promote and spread the glory, and the honor of Satan in the world. He is the one who is influencing man to do things reflecting the glory of Satan such as lying, killing, stealing, listening to profane music. On Wednesday: Another minister of Satan work and his mission is to spread pride and self-consideration in the world. (Me myself and I). On Thursday: another demon work and his mission to spread division in the Body of Christ and the churches and within families. His mission in connected to Satan's fifth commandments. On Friday: Another demon work and his mission is to spread the apostasy in the church and thus turn man against the works of God and submit them to the riches of this world and the authority of this world. On Saturday: Another demon work and his mission are in twofold: the first part is to make man rebellious and stubborn. It's this demon who makes man not to obey or yield to advices until they see the consequences. The second part of his mission is to push man toward the celebrity status and lifestyle. Man having earring, tattoo because they saw one celebrity or a musician doing the same. This demon works with another demon which is the demon of music. On Sunday, the demon who works is Akiel, the demon of poverty. It is he who is influencing and pushes man not to make a financial offering to God. Satan loves poverty and his goal is to keep God's children in poverty. Poverty makes people to go toward Satan. One became easily a witch, wizard because of poverty. One became a robber a murderer, because of poverty; one became jealous because of poverty. Poverty is a huge weapon that Satan uses to enticed man to his camp. Within Satan' army, they are Satanic and Satanists. The Satanic are the fallen angels those who were kicked out of heaven with Satan himself. But the Satanists are human beings who work for Satan.

Brothers, I write you about this topic briefly and I know in reading this, someone could say, Patrick, it doesn't sound to me that any of the things that you're talking about will stop a mugger from mugging you? All you're talking about is spiritual things, I will answer you that the reason I'm talking about spiritual thing is because the weapons of our warfare are not carnal, but they are mighty through God to the pulling down of strongholds. A whole lot of time we think folks are our problems, in this world today, no individual is your problem but there is a spirit, an evil spirit that's running ramping through the earth that's causing man to fight their neighbors, causing nations to declared war on other nations, because you understand that we wrestle not against flesh and blood but against principalities, against powers, against the rulers of the darkness of this world, against spiritual wickedness in the high places. Now, who are these? These are the ranks of Satan's kingdom and any military man will tell you that when you break the first line of defense, you haven't won the war, you have to move on further and break through another line and if you want to fight Satan and battle against evil, you have to armed yourself, and to be able to do that, you have to be strong in the Lord and in the power of His might, you have to put on the whole armor of God so that you may be able to stand firm against the tactics of the devil, therefore, put on the whole armor of God, that you may be able to resist the evil day and, having done everything, to hold your ground. So stand fast with your loins girded in truth, clothed with righteousness as a breastplate, and your feet shod in the readiness for the gospel of peace. In all circumstances, hold faith as a shield, to quench all the flaming arrows fiery darts of the evil one. And take the helmet of salvation and the sword of the Spirit, which is the Word of God and be sober and vigilant, for your opponent the devil is prowling around like a roaring lion looking for someone to devour. Resist him, steadfast in faith, knowing that your fellow believers throughout the world undergo the same sufferings.

The problem of evil is still pressing and still unavoidable, and no quick answer will suffice especially for those who experience or have experienced pain and suffering. Only the Christian faith as a whole provides a way to overcome evil and suffering. This is one of the causes of our hope, nothing is so evil that God cannot cause a good to come from it: "We know that all things work together for good for those who love God" (Romans 8:28). All the saints affirm this truth.

Part Two

THE FALL OF MAN

Therefore, rejoice you heavens, and you who dwell in them. But woe to you, Earth and Sea, for Lucifer/ Satan has come down to you in great fury, for he knows he has but a short time.

Revelation 12:12

Genesis

I n the beginning God created the heaven and the earth. And the earth was without form, and void; and darkness was upon the face of the deep. And the Spirit of God moved upon the face of the waters. And God said, let there be light; and there was light. And God saw the light that it was good, and God divided the light from the darkness. And God called the light Day, and the darkness he called Night. Thus evening came, and morning followed. The first day.

And God said, let there be a firmament in the midst of the waters, and let it divide the waters from the waters. And God made the firmament, and divided the waters which were under the firmament from the waters which were above the firmament, and it was so. And God called the firmament Heaven. Evening came and morning followed. The second day.

And God said, let the waters under the heaven be gathered together unto one place, and let dry land appear: and it was so. And God called the dry land Earth, and the gathering together of the waters God called Seas. And God saw that it was good. And God said, let the earth bring forth grass, the herb yielding seed, and the fruit tree yielding fruit after his kind, whose seed is in itself, upon the earth: and it was so. And the earth brought forth grass and herb yielding seed after his kind, and the tree yielding fruit, whose seed was in itself, after his kind: and God saw that it was good. Evening came, and morning followed. The third day.

And God said, let there be lights in the firmament of the heaven to divide the day from the night; and let them be for signs, and for seasons, and for days, and years; And let them be for lights in the firmament of the heaven to give light upon the earth: and it was so. And God made two great lights; the greater light to rule the day, and the lesser light to rule the night, and God made the stars also. God set them in the firmament of the heaven to give light upon the earth, and to rule over the day and over the night, and divide the light from the darkness: and God saw that it was good. Evening came, and morning followed. The fourth day.

And God said, let the waters bring forth abundantly the moving creature that hath life, and fowl that may fly above the earth in the open firmament of heaven. and God created great whales, and every living creature that moveth, which the waters brought forth abundantly, after their kind, and every winged fowl after his kind: and God saw that it was good. And God blessed them, saying, Be fruitful, and multiply, and fill the waters in the seas, and let fowl multiply in the earth. Evening came, and morning followed. The fifth day.

And God said, let the earth bring forth the living creature after his kind, cattle, and creeping thing, and beast of the earth after his kind: and it was so. And God made the beast of the earth after his kind, and cattle after their kind, and every thing that creepth upon the earth after his kind: and God saw that it was good. And God said, let us make man in our image, after our likeness: and let them have dominion over the fish of the sea, and over the fowl of the air, and over the cattle, and over all the earth, and over every creepy thing that creepth upon the earth. so God created man in his own image, in the image of God created he him, male and female created he them. And God blessed them, and God said unto them, Be fruitful, and multiply, and replenish the earth, and subdue it: and have dominion over the fish of the sea, and over the fowl of the air, and over every living thing that moveth upon the earth. and God said, behold, I have given you every hear bearing seed, which is upon the face of all the earth, and every tree, in the which is the fruit of a tree yielding seed; to you it shall be for meat. And to every beast of the earth, and to every fowl of the air, and to every thing that creepth upon the earth, wherein there is life, I have given every green herb for meat: and it was so. And God saw every thing that He had made, and, behold, it was very good. Evening came, and morning followed. The sixth day.

Thus the heavens and the earth were finished, and all the host of them. And on the seventh day God ended his work which he had made; and he rested on the seventh day, and sanctified it: because that in it He has rested from all his work which God created and made. These are the generations of the heavens and of the earth when they were created, in the day that the Lord God made the earth and the heavens. And every plant of the field before it was in the earth, and every herb of the field before it grew; for the Lord God had not caused it to rain upon the earth, and there was not a man to till the ground. But there went up a mist from the earth, and watered the whole face of the ground (Genesis 1-2:1-7)

The Garden of Eden

And the Lord God planted a garden eastward in Eden; and there he put the man whom He had formed. And out of the ground made the Lord God to grow every tree that is pleasant to the sight, and good for food; the tree of life also in the midst of the garden, and the tree of knowledge of good and evil. And a river went out of eden to water the garden; and from thence it was parted, and became into four heads. The name of the first is Pison; that is it which compasseth the whole land of Havilah, where there is gold. And the gold of that land is good there is bdellium and the onyx stone. And the name of the second river is Gihon; the same is that compasseth the whole land of Ethiopia. And the name of the third river is Hiddekel; that is it which goeth toward the east of Assyria. And the fourth river is Euphrates. And the Lord God took the man, and put him into the Garden of Eden to dress it, cultivate it and to keep it. And the Lord God gave man this order: "You are free to eat from any of the trees of the garden except the tree of knowledge of good and evil. From that tree you shall not eat; the moment you eat from it you are surely doomed to die." And the Lord God said, it is not good that the man should be alone: I will make him an help meet for him. And out of the ground the Lord God formed every beast of the field, and every fowl of the air; and brought them unto Adam to see what he would call them; and whatsoever Adam called every living creature, that was the name thereof. And Adam gave names to all cattle, and to the fowl of the air, and to every beast of the field; but for Adam there was not found an help meet for him. And the Lord God caused a deep sleep to fall upon Adam, and he slept; and he took one of his ribs, and closed up the flesh instead thereof; and the rib, which the Lord God had taken from man, made he a woman, and brought her unto the man. And Adam said, this is now bone of my bones, and flesh of my flesh: she shall be called Woman, because she was taken out of Man. Therefore shall a man leave his father and his mother, and shall cleave unto his wife and they shall be one flesh. And they were both naked, the man and his wife, and were not ashamed. (Genesis 2:8-25).

The Test & Temptation

Now the serpent was the most cunning, the most subtle of all the animals that the Lord God had made. The serpent asked the woman, "Did God really tell you not to eat from any of the trees in the garden?" The woman answered the serpent: "We may eat of the fruit of the trees in the garden, but of the fruit of the tree which is in the midst of the garden that God said, 'You shall not eat it or even touch it, lest you die. But the serpent said unto the woman: "You certainly will not die! No, God knows well that the moment you eat of it, your eyes will be opened and you will be like gods, knowing what is good and what is evil. (Genesis 3:1-5)

The Fall of Man

And when the woman saw that the tree was good for food, pleasing to the eyes, and desirable for gaining wisdom, she took of the fruit thereof, and did eat, and gave also unto her husband who was with her, and he ate it. Then the eyes of both of them were opened, and they realized that they were naked; so they sewed fig leaves together, and made loincloths for themselves. When they heard the sound of the Lord God moving about in the garden at the breezy time of the day, Adam and his wife hid themselves from the presence of the Lord God among the trees of the garden. And the Lord God called unto Adam, and asked him, "Where are you?" He answered. "I heard you in the garden; but I was afraid, because I was naked, so I hid myself." Then God asked, "Who told you that you were naked? You have eaten, then, from the tree of which I forbidden you to eat!" Adam replied, "The woman whom you gave to be with me, she gave me fruit of the tree, and so I did eat." The Lord God then asked the woman, "Why did you do such a thing?" The woman answered, "The serpent deceived, beguiled and tricked me into it, so I ate it." (Genesis 3:6-13)

The Curse

Then the Lord God said to the serpent: "Because you have done this, you are cursed, you shall be banned from all the animals and from all the wild creatures; on your belly shall you crawl, and dirt shall you eat all the days of your life. I will put enmity between you and the woman, and between your offspring and hers; He will strike at your head, while you strike at his heel. To the woman God said, "I will multiply your sorrow and multiply the pangs of your childbearing; in pain shall you bring forth children and your desire and urge shall be for your husband, and he shall rule over you and be your master." To Adam God said: "Because you hearkened unto the voice of your wife, and ate from the tree of which I had forbidden you to eat, "Cursed is the ground because of you! In toil and sorrow you shall eat its yield all the days of your life. Thorns and thistles shall it bring forth to you, as you eat of the plants of the field. By the sweat of your face shall you get bread to eat, until you return to the ground from which you were taken; for you are dirt, and to dirt you shall return."

And Adam called his wife's name Eve; because she was the mother of all the living. Unto Adam also and to his wife did the Lord God make coats of skins, leather garments with which He clothed them. (Genesis 3:14-21)

Separation from God

Then the Lord God said, "Behold, the man is become as one of us, to know what is good and what is evil! And now, lest he put forth his hand, and take also of the tree of life, and eat, and live forever: The Lord God therefore banished him from the Garden of Eden and sent him forth from the garden to till the ground from which he had been taken. So he drove out the man, and when he expelled him, man settled east of the Garden of Eden and God stationed the cherubim and the fiery revolving sword which turned every way, to guard and keep the way of the tree of life. (Genesis 3:22-24)

Death Reigns

We meet the specter early, in Genesis 2. In order to give man freedom to be a responsible moral being, God placed a certain tree in the center of the Garden and commanded man not to eat. With the command came warning of the consequences: "When you eat of it you will surely die" (v.17). This opportunity to eat was no trap, or even a test. Given the intention of God that man should be in His own image, that the tree was a necessity! There is no moral dimension to the existence of a robot; it can only respond to the program imposed by its maker. Robots have no capacity to value, no ability to choose between good and bad, or good and better. To be truly like God, man must have the freedom to make moral choices and the opportunity to choose, however great the risk such freedom may involve. Daily Adam and Eve may have passed that tree, gladly obeying a God they knew and trusted. Until finally a third being stepped in.

With Genesis 3 there come a shattering of the idyllic picture of man in Eden. With a sudden jolt the harmony of original Creation is torn with discord; a wild cacophony of sounds among which we can hear notes of anger, jealousy, pride, disobedience, murder, and the accompanying inner agonies of pain and shame and guilt. God's creation of man as a person stands as the source of good in us; now we face the source of evil. The fall of man is described in genesis 3; Genesis 4 is included to help us realize the consequences of the fall and the implications of the spiritual death that grips humanity. Yet even this dark message is brightened by the promise contained in God's continued love, and in history's first sacrifice.

We see death in the sudden flush of shame that spread as Adam and Eve recognized their nakedness (Gen 3:7). Today the more "mature" defend public nakedness as morally neutral. "Evil is in the eye of the beholder," is the phrase they often use to attack anyone who objects, never realizing how condemning that excuse is. Evil is in the eye of the beholder, not in the creation of God. But since the Fall, the eye is evil! We see death demonstrated in the first pair's flight from Good. They had known His love, yet awareness of guilt alienated them from Him, and they tried to hide. We see death in Adam's refusal to accept responsibility for his choice. He tried to shift the blame, first to Eve, and then ultimately to God Himself. "It was the woman You gave me who brought me some, it's her fault." We see death in judgment on earth for man's sake. Most of all, we see death in the anger of Cain, whose bitterness led him to murder his own brother, Abed. How deeply that tragedy must have driven home to Adam and Eve the implications of their choice. Father and mother must have stood in tears, gazing at the fallen body of one son, knowing only too well that the hand of their older boy was crimson with his blood. We see death in the civilization that sprang up as the family of man multiplied. Lamech broke the pattern of man/woman relationship which God had ordained: "The two shall become one flesh" (Gen 2:24). Not only did Lamech commit bigamy, but he boldly justified the murder of another man who had in some way injured him. Actually, we hardly need repeated proofs. Each day's headlines bring us new testimony. The wrong we choose, the guilt and shame we bear, the way we strike out to hurt and to harm, are ever-present internal witnesses to Eden's loss. Yes, how well man knows good and evil now!

The Earth is Cursed

And the Lord God said to Adam

"Because you hearkened unto the voice of your wife, and ate from the tree of which I had forbidden you to eat, "Cursed is the ground because of you! In toil and sorrow you shall eat its yield all the days of your life. Thorns and thistles shall it bring forth to you, as you eat of the plants of the field. By the sweat of your face shall you get bread to eat, until you return to the ground from which you were taken; for you are dirt, and to dirt you shall return." (Genesis 3:17-19)

The story of man goes with Adam; Adam had relations with his wife Eve, and Eve conceived and bore Cain, next she bore his brother Abel. Cain attacked his bother Abel and killed him, why did he slaughter him? Because Cain belonged to the evil one and that Cain own works were evil, and those of his brother righteous. (1John 3:12).

The earth opened its mouth to receive the blood of the righteous Abel from the hand of Cain. By the time we get to chapter 6 of Genesis, men began to multiply on earth and daughters were born of them but when the Lord saw how great man's wickedness on earth was, and how no desire that his heart conceived was ever anything but evil, the Lord regretted that He had made man on the earth, and His heart was grieved. Then the Lord decided to bring judgment on the whole earth. And God said: "I will empty the earth and make it desolate and lay it waste, I will twist its surface, turn it upside down, and scatter its inhabitant. The earth shall be utterly plundered. The earth mourns and fades, the world languishes and withers. The earth is polluted because of its inhabitants, the highest people of the earth languish, the earth is defiled under its inhabitants for they have transgressed the laws, violated the statutes, broken the everlasting covenant, therefore a curse devours the earth, and its inhabitants pay and suffer their guilt. Therefore, the inhabitants of the earth are scorched and turn pale, and few man are left. Terror, pit, trap and snare are upon the inhabitants of the earth, for the windows of heaven are opened, and the foundation of the earth tremble and shake. The earth burst asunder and is utterly broken; the earth is shaken apart and will be split, the earth is convulsed and staggers like a drunken man, it sways like a hut. Its transgression and rebellion lies heavy upon it and weigh it down until it falls, and will not rise again.

The Lord will punish the hosts of heavens in the heavens, and the kings of the earth on the earth. They will be gathered together like prisoners into a pit. They will be shut up in a dungeon, and after many days they will be punished. Then the moon will blush and be confounded and the sun will be ashamed and will grow pale, for the Lord of hosts will reign on Mount Zion and in Jerusalem, glorious in the sight of his elders.

Future Glory

I consider that the sufferings of this present time are as nothing to be compared with the glory to be revealed for us. For the creation waits with eager longing expectation the revelation of the sons of God. For creation was made subject to futility, not of its own accord but because of the one who subjected it, in hope that creation itself would be set free from slavery to corruption and its bondage to decay and share in the glorious freedom of the children of God. We know that all creation is groaning in labor pains even until now; and not only that, but we ourselves, who have the first fruits of the Spirit, we also groan within ourselves as we wait for adoption, the redemption of our bodies.

Part Three

SIN & INIQUITY

Behold, I was brought forth in iniquity, and in sin
did my mother conceive me

Isaiah 51:5

What is Sin?

The Bible teaches us that sin is a transgression of the law, (1John 3:4) that, all unrighteousness is sin (1John 5:17), and everything that does not come from faith is sin (Romans 14:23), whoever knows the right thing to do and fails to do it, for him it is sin (James 4:17).

There are three primary words for "sin" in the Hebrew language. Each of them implies the existence of a standard of righteousness established by God. One of the three, *hata,'* means to "miss the mark," or "fall short of the divine standard." *Pesa'* is usually rendered by "rebellion" or "transgression," and indicates revolt against the standard. *'Awon*, translated by "iniquity" or "guilt," is a twisting of the standard or deviation from it."

Separation from God

Behold, the LORD'S hand is not shortened, that it cannot save; neither his ear heavy, that it cannot hear: but your iniquities have separated between you and your God, and your sins have hid his face from you, that he will not hear. For your hands are defiled with blood, and your fingers with iniquity; your lips have spoken lies, your tongue hath muttered perverseness. None calleth for justice, nor any pleadeth for truth: they trust in vanity, and speak lies; they conceive mischief, and bring forth iniquity. They hatch cockatrice' eggs, and weave the spider's web: he that eateth of their eggs dieth, and that which is crushed breaketh out into a viper. Their webs shall not become garments, neither shall they cover themselves with their works: their works are works of iniquity, and the act of violence is

29

in their hands. Their feet run to evil, and they make haste to shed innocent blood: their thoughts are thoughts of iniquity; wasting and destruction are in their paths. The way of peace they know not; and there is no judgment in their goings: they have made them crooked paths: whosoever goeth therein shall not know peace.

Therefore is judgment far from us, neither doth justice overtake us: we wait for light, but behold obscurity; for brightness, but we walk in darkness. We grope for the wall like the blind, and we grope as if we had no eyes: we stumble at noonday as in the night; we are in desolate places as dead men. We roar all like bears, and mourn sore like doves: we look for judgment, but there is none; for salvation, but it is far off from us. For our transgressions are multiplied before thee, and our sins testify against us: for our transgressions are with us; and as for our iniquities, we know them; in transgressing and lying against the LORD, and departing away from our God, speaking oppression and revolt, conceiving and uttering from the heart words of falsehood. And judgment is turned away backward, and justice standeth afar off: for truth is fallen in the street, and equity cannot enter. Yea, truth faileth; and he that departeth from evil maketh himself a prey: and the LORD saw it, and it displeased him that there was no judgment. And he saw that there was no man, and wondered that there was no intercessor: therefore his arm brought salvation unto him; and his righteousness, it sustained him. For he put on righteousness as a breastplate, and an helmet of salvation upon his head; and he put on the garments of vengeance for clothing, and was clad with zeal as a cloke. According to their deeds, accordingly he will repay, fury to his adversaries, recompense to his enemies; to the islands he will repay recompense. So shall they fear the name of the LORD from the west, and his glory from the rising of the sun. When the enemy shall come in like a flood, the Spirit of the LORD shall lift up a standard against him.

And the Redeemer shall come to Zion, and unto them that turn from transgression in Jacob, saith the LORD. As for me, this is my covenant with them, saith the LORD; My spirit that is upon thee, and my words which I have put in thy mouth, shall not depart out of thy mouth, nor out of the mouth of thy seed, nor out of the mouth of thy seed's seed, saith the LORD, from henceforth and for ever. (Isaiah 59:1-21)

Sin of Adam to all Man

Lucifer, with a great number of angelic beings who followed him, was judged in a titanic fall. Lucifer's name was changed to Satan, and from his arrogance was born an unending hatred of God. It was this being, this great adversary of God and His people, who came in the dawning of the world in the guise of a serpent, to tempt Eve and deceived her. He isolated Eve from Adam, he gave the pair no opportunity to strengthen each other in a resolve of choose the good. Then he cast out doubt on God's motives. Did God possibly have a selfish motive for the restriction? (Gen 3:4) Satan went on to contradict God. God had warned of death; Satan cried, "That's a lie!" Now two opposing views stood in sharp contrast, and a choice had to be made. Led along by the tempter, Eve made her choice. She rejected trust in God and confidence in His wisdom and, as Satan himself had before her, Eve determined to follow her own will and reject God's. Then she offered the fruit to Adam, and he too ate. After Adam and Eve had made their choice and had eaten the forbidden fruit, they suddenly realized what they had done. They did know good and evil! But, unlike God, their knowledge came from a personal experience of the wrong. With wide open eyes they looked at each other and, for the first time, looked away in shame.

Sin entered the world through one man, and death through sin, and in this way death came to all man, because all sinned." (Romans 5:12).

The life of the body is in the blood, the blood runs through every vein in the body, every part of your body has a vein in it, and what keeps that vein going is the blood that flows through the body, blood is important and this is why we must look at the importance of Jesus' communion because, it shows forth the death and the sufferings of Lord Jesus till He comes. All of us blood was contaminated and affected from the fruit of the tree at the garden, Adam immediately contacted blood poisoning and started to die a slow death, because when the blood of Adam became poison his body was affected, there was no time before man sin against God, there was no killing before man's sin against God, but when Adam sinned everything went into motion, his blood was contaminated with sin and became poisoned and all of us who came from Adam, our blood is affected and poisoned and thus inherited Adam's sin nature and suffered the same consequences of spiritual and physical death. But God in His infinite love, set the plan of redemption right away and he set it on the wheels of time and time began to move on, because it became necessary for God to send a redeemer, and the word redeem means to come back, and that's why God sent Jesus for, to bring us back into fellowship, with our Maker, because before sin entered into the world, man had fellowship with God, we had communion with Him but it was all because of sin that caused man to separate from God but I'm so glad that God has made a way for us, to have fellowship with Him, and it is through the blood of Jesus. Jesus, the Son of God, born of a virgin woman but conceived by the Holy Spirit, he came to redeemed us back to our God, we were lost in sin, we weren't fit to live, and we were ready to die.

The implications of Adam's sin have caused the human personality to warped and marred. The image of God dimmed and twisted. Man was ruled by death and all that death implies. What heritage had Adam to pass on to humanity? Only what he has. He fathered a son in his image: a son who, like Adam, had worth and value because of his correspondence to the Divine, but who, like Adam, lived in chains. "Therefore just as sin entered the world through one man, and death through sin and in this way death came to all men, because all sinned."

All sin has consequences beyond the initial wrongdoing. Sin always has undesirable effects on those around us. The ripples of Adam's momentous sin are still being felt. Jesus took the death that was our penalty upon Him, He took our sufferings on His body and suffered for our sins "so that in Him we might become the righteousness of God."

Sin & Consequences

God placed Adam in a wonderful environment, a beautiful garden and provided for all his needs. God gave him work to engage his mind and his hands, provided a life-partner for him, had personal fellowship with him, and warned him of the consequences of disobedience. Yet Adam sinned. Adam was given one specific law by God to obey, and Adam chose to disobey this revealed will of God.

The first human sin involved the choice of self-interests rather than God's interests, the making of self the chief end rather than God, and the rejection of God as the highest authority with Adam putting his own authority above God's. The first consequence of Adam and Eve's sin was the suffering of guilt, their soul were troubled, their conscience were no longer at peace, they began to suffer emotionally and that guilt expressed itself in two ways, they suffered shame and they suffered fear. Satan promised enlightement, he had left out a vital part of the truth: that they would be reminded of good without having the power to do it, and that they would know evil without having the power to avoid it. Then came condemnation. Eve to suffer sorrow and subjection, and Adam to suffer a life of painful toil and finally they suffered the separation from the garden and from fellowship with God.

The original sin caused God's creation to become corrupt and to go bad a=has profound philosophical and theological implications. Sin brought not only death to human but a host of other changes, including weeds, pain, cruelty, suffering, earthquakes, flood, hurricanes, tornadoes, lightning strikes, volcanic eruptions, tsunamis, droughts, blizzards, and impacts by meteorites, asteroids, and cornets. Etc.

In conclusion, we can resume that all bad things in the world are the result of Adam and Eve original sin. Sin resulted in judgment and death. The earth is cursed and therefore sin resulted in animals and human death, the growth of weeds, animals becoming carnivorous, and all manner of diseases and natural disasters. In essence, Adam is blamed for everything bad in the world, relieving God, relieving God of the blame for all the suffering. When God finished His creation, he pronounced it very good. So why do we suffer now? We see suffering all around us today, something must have happened to change creation-that something was sin. A world of pain, cruelty, suffering, and death is the result of Satan's constant influence on man to commit sin, and not of God's love. This is also an attempt to and "answer" atheist's charges that there is too much evil in the world for a good God to exist.

Now we understand that Satan is the author of sin. Sin is the reason that we have afflictions, including death. All of our problems and our suffering, including death itself, are a result of man's rebellion against God. Man said, "I don't need You, God. I can build my world without You." God said, "If you take that position, you will suffer and die." Man took that position, and he began to suffer, and he has been dying ever since. Physical death is just the death of the body, but the spirit lives on. If your spirit is separated from God for eternity, it will be lost forever. But the great news is that God has provided a rescue in the Person of His Son, Jesus Christ. That's why Christ died on the cross, and that's why He rose from the dead.

Part Four

POLITICS
BAD GOVERNMENT & BAD
ADMINISTRATION

When the Lord saw how great was man's wickedness on earth, that every imagination of his thoughts
and no desire that his heart conceived was ever anything but evil, He regretted that He had made man
on the earth, and His heart was grieved.

Genesis 6:5-6

The Love of Money is the Root of Evil (Causes of Division)

W here comes wars and where do the conflicts among you come from? It is not from your own lust and your passions that make war within your members? You covet but do not possess. You kill and envy but you cannot obtain; you fight and wage war. You do not possess because you do not ask. You ask but do not receive, because you ask wrongly, to spend it on your passions. (James 4). For we brought nothing into the world, just as we shall not be able to take anything out of it. If we have food and clothing, we shall be content with that. Those who want to be rich are falling into temptation and into a trap and into many foolish and harmful desires, which plunge them into ruin and destruction. For the love of money is the root of all evils, and some people in their desire for it have strayed from the faith and have pierced themselves with many pains. But you avoid all this. Instead, pursue righteousness, devotion, faith, love, patience, and gentleness. (1Timothy 6:7-11).

"Money," is of no value in itself (the paper or the metal). It is desirable only because it is a cultural symbol which can be traded for the "many desires" that we have. But it cannot be traded for God or godliness. And because of the fact that money is a cultural symbol which can be traded for, and man puts values on it, money has become literally an idol for many people, and God hates idolatry and idolaters. Therefore, the love of money corresponds to the root longing for the things money can buy minus God. That is why all these {many desires} "plunge people into ruin and destruction." Good desires don't destroy. Only desires for anything minus

God destroy. That is why the love of money represents. Therefore, this love is the root of all evils that men commit. Because all evils come from that root desire, the desire for anything minus God. No exceptions. This is the essence of sin and the root of all sinning-falling short of the glory of God. Or, to put it another way, sin is: exchanging God for the creation. In other words, at root, sin is preferring anything above God. "All evils" come from this preferring, or this desiring. If something is desired for God's sake, that desire is not sin. If anything is desired not for God's sake, not to glorify God, that desire is sin. Therefore, all sin, "all evils,: come from this desire. It is through the love of money that some have wandered away from the faith. The love of money works its destruction by luring the soul to forsake faith. Faith is the contend trust in Christ, for godliness with contentment is great gain. Faith says, "I have learned in whatever situation I am to be content. Faith has contentment in all circumstances because it has Christ, and Christ makes up every loss: "I count everything as loss because of the surpassing worth of knowing Christ Jesus my Lord." All true virtue grows from this root of resting in Christ. Without it, we perform our deeds not as an expression of Christ all-sufficiency, but in order to make up for some deficiency we feel, for lack of faith. But that is not true virtue, and it doesn't honor Christ. Only what is done from faith is truly virtuous. "For whatever does not proceed from faith is sin." Which means, "All evils" rise from the soul that has been lured away from faith. And that is what the love of money does. Through this love of money "some have wandered away from the faith." But "without faith it is impossible to please God." Only evil comes from faithlessness-all evil.

Bad Government & Bad Administration

Have you ever wondered why there is war, why there is poverty, division and crime? There is a reason for it all, everything is done on purpose. Why if I told you, that those corrupting the world, poisoning our food and igniting conflict were themselves about to be permanently eradicated from the earth? Let me tell you, there are real criminals out there, we need to just recognize our true enemy and I am not talking about those criminals we acknowledge, of course, they rob our houses, steal our cars, steal our phones, murder us too if they think they can get away with it. We all experienced criminals in one way or another. Criminals as we know are those who choose personal gain over the right of others with no regards for laws. But let me tell you, criminals can also succeed in business and politics, and can be elected as our leaders. {Imagine a criminal becoming the President? Imagine what they could achieve!} They could use the full weight of their executive power to commit much larger crimes, and ensure they and their friends were enriched to the fullest extent possible. A criminal president could create alliances with other criminal presidents, and then collaborate on more global criminal activities, and anything goes (drug-running, human trafficking, whatever makes the big bucks.)

The 20th century was turbulent as Jesus predicted with war, economic disaster, famines and displacement, we have accepted these things as just human nature and simply the way the world works, something inevitable and due to the weakness of human nature that lead us to these actions and suffering. You see, this is where we are all tragically wrong, it's a mind control, they use the mainstream media to brain wash us, you are not a criminal- I am not a criminal. They are the criminals, they are joins people into their way of thinking, and into their way of perception, the way they want us to think and perceive. Who are they, how they do it, what they want, how did it start? They got power, they rose to the top of media companies that control our news and entertainment. They ascended to the top of the banking system, also to the Oval Office, to Brussel, to the Vatican, to the Crown (UK). They crept in quietly they becomes leaders of agricultural companies who have control over food supply, also big pharmaceutical companies; the ones we trust to help us when we are sick. Nobody stopped them and they just recruited more criminals to help them. First they accumulated the world's wealth; they invented a system of money called central banking which lends money to governments with interest, placing countries into eternal debt. People's wealth got less and their wealth got more. Much more. They diverted attention to their last remaining competitor. The people of the world namely you & me. They use their control of the media to set black against white, woman against man, young against old, Muslim against Christian. They convinced us we are the problem so that we would fight and destroy ourselves. To get it done faster, they attacked all aspect of humanity that make us strong like family, using their influence over culture, they popularized lifestyle choices that led to a surge in broken homes, lost youth and substance abuse. They create a wholesome conservative female role model that parents encourage their daughter to admire then mutate values away from conservatism to distort female sexuality ruining marriage and family. They deliberately weakened us when we are just trying to get on with living.

So where are all the good guys? Good people just want to get married, have kids, make a living and enjoy their liberty. John Kennedy was a good guy, he knew about them and wanted them gone, he said before is assassination "There is a plot in this country to enslave every man, woman, and child. Before I leave this high and noble office, I intend to expose this plot." He knew their intention for us all and he wanted to fight them. Sadly he had no idea how powerful they had become. These criminals are also known as the Deep State, or Cabal, because of how they control things behind the scenes. With each bad president came a new depths America and the world would sink. The world collapsed into darkness. You would ask me how? They destroyed factories, declining jobs numbers, sicker people, opioids, destruction of Iraq, Syria and

Yemen with pointless war, displacement of people into Europe, Isis, Terrorism, collapsed government, poverty and genocide. Total suffering and misery.

This is the result of what a bad government and a bad administration can do; they purposely create calamities and bring sufferings in the world. The effects of Bad Government, crime is rampant and diseased citizen roam a crumbling city. The countryside suffers from drought. Bad Government has its effects on the citizen of the country, and on the life of the cities and villages. Lorenzetti's "Allegory of Good and Bad Government" is a reminder that good government is characterized by Justice, Concord, Peace, and Wisdom while bad government is animated by Division, Avarice, Fury, Vainglory, even Tyranny. When good government reigns, all is well. When bad government plagues the realm, the Tyrant usurps the power of the people and the citizens suffer.

Part Five

SPIRITUAL PRINCIPLES

Make no mistake, be not deceived; God is not
mocked: for whatsoever a person sow, that will he
also reap.

Galatians 6:7

The Spiritual Principle of Sowing & Reaping

S owing and reaping is a spiritual principle like any other spiritual law, and it holds significant way in the world we live in. it helps us live a fruitful life if we choose the good. The spiritual principle of sowing and reaping will work for everyone under the right conditions. When you fulfil its terms, it will produce results for you. This has scriptural basis in the word of God according to Galatians 6:7-8; which read, "Be not deceived; God is not mocked: for whatsoever a man soweth, that shall he also reap. For he that soweth to his flesh shall of the flesh reap corruption; but he that soweth to the spirit shall of the spirit reap life everlasting."

Sowing and reaping is a law of the natural world. Sowing is the simplest (and often the least expensive) way to bring introduces new plants into the garden; it is the act of scattering seeds on land so that they may grow. Sowing is a process of starting something, contrary to reaping which is the process of receiving something. Your life and the environment that surrounded you is like a garden, and everyday through your actions, your words, or your deeds whether or not you realize it, you are sowing in that garden, now, whatever you sow is a seed. What kind of seeds are you sowing? Your thoughts are seed, your words are seed, your actions are seed. Whatever becomes of your life, what become of you, is first sowed in your mind and in your heart. Bad seed produces bad fruit; and good seed produces good fruits.

The Spiritual Principle of the Seed

A seed is a fertilized grain and as such is a living thing, but in a dormant state, which requires being in a suitable matter to trigger off. It's a tiny beginning with a huge future or consequence. A seed is anything that can become more. It is the beginning, it is anything you can do, know, say, or possess that could bless or curse somebody else. For instances, your thoughts are seeds for desired behavior, conduct or creativity. Your word is a seed, doing good or evil is a seed, your love is a seed, your hatred is a seed, your knowledge is a seed, your ignorance is a seed, your money is a seed, your kindness is a seed, your temper is a seed, your jealousy is a seed, stopping slander is a seed. Everything is a seed. Your seed is anything you have received, whether from God or from the evil one and it can be traded for something else. You are a walking warehouse of seeds. Most people do not even know this; they have no idea how many seeds they contain that can be planted into the lives of others. Anything that improves another is a seed, anything that makes another cry is a seed, and anything that makes someone's life easier or harder is a seed.

It is very crucial to inventory your needs, but it is more important to inventory your seeds. Little things birth big things. You are a living collection of seeds, your seed is any gift, skills or talent that God has provided for you to sow into the lives of others around you.

Most people have no idea about what a seed really is. Showing up at the work late....is a seed. Showing up earlier at work is another seed. You see, anything that you can do make life easier for anyone else...is a seed. Your seed is any gifts, skill or talent that God has provided for you to sow into the lives of others around you. Use your seed knowing that bad seed produces bad fruits. The Bible says that the works of the flesh are obvious: immorality, impurity, licentiousness, idolatry, sorcery, hatreds, rivalry, jealousy, outbursts of fury, acts of selfishness, dissensions, factions, occasions of envy, drinking bouts, orgies, and the like. I warn you, that those who do and practice such things will not inherit the kingdom of God. (Galatians 5:19-21). When the Bible talks about the works of the flesh, it's not referring to our body, this is about our mind and the way we reason, our thoughts process, anything outside of the influence of God and the inspiration of the Word of God by the Holy Spirit. Therefore, when you sow to your flesh, it means that when disaster strikes, you look to the world for solutions. Sowing to the flesh is about being dominated by negativity. When you reap corruption, it means that you are not in alignment to God's master plan and blueprint for your life, so you are not getting the best of your investment because it is fleshly rather than spiritual.

Now let me ask you this, what kinds of thought dominates your mind every day? Negative thoughts leads to negative communication, which in turn leads to negative actions. You manifest to the outside world that which is inside you. This was a principle showed by Jesus in the gospel according to St Luke 6:45, it says: "A good man out of the good treasure of his heart bringeth forth that which is good; and evil man out of the evil treasure of his heart bringeth forth that which is evil; for of the abundance of the heart his mouth speakth." Racism is a seed, violence is a seed, discord is a seed, sadism is a seed, covetousness is a seed, lying is a seed, animosity is a seed, disrespect is a seed, greed is a seed, murder is a seed, and the like are contributors of the sufferings of this world.

The word of God is the seed you need, because it is incorruptible and it is life. When you have more and more of it, you will not harvest corruption. In other words, your life will be more and more powerful and Christ like. Your mind will not be corrupted by the thinking of this world.

You can never harvest a orange from a lemon seed.

The Spiritual Principle of Cause & Effect

Human being, according to the laws of nature, must pay for all their wrong actions, but when we tune ourselves to God and His word, we see then the perfect image of Christ within us. Then we realize who we really are in Christ, and we need not suffer for our past errors. But if we again became identified with our sinful nature by not forgiving others, then we again subject ourselves to be governed by the exacting law of cause and effect.

The law of cause of effect is defined by actions, whether physical or mental, individual or performed by a group, and each action has a consequence. The law of cause and effect can also affect a group of people such as a religion, country, or even a planet. A country can be conquered, or have droughts or famine, because that was the overall consequences of the group, even if a few did not have that consequences. Very few people realize how many of their actions and desires are generated by the seed they sowed in the past. They believe they are acting on free will, but instead they are acting out habits buried deep in their subconscious mind from many past lifetimes. If you sow evil, you will reap evil in the form of suffering. And if you sow goodness, you will reap goodness, peace, happiness in a form of inner joy.

Every action, every thought, brings about its own corresponding rewards. Human suffering is neither a sign of God's anger with mankind nor God's lack of love with mankind. It is a sign, rather, of man's ignorance of the divine law of man's refusal to obey God's commandments. We must understand how our intentions, motives, desires, and the emotional drive with which we conduct our actions have an effect on our lives and how they are related to the law of sowing and reaping and the law of cause and effect. Everything that one encounters is one's own design; nobody else is responsible for it. Of course they are few exceptions to this reality but, overall, for endless lives, one has been responsible, wholly and solely. Intent and an action of an individual (cause) influence the future of that individual (effect). Good intent and good deeds contribute to a future happiness, while evil intent and evil deeds contribute to bad future suffering.

Part Six

THE ABSENCE OF LOVE IS THE PRESENCE OF EVIL

For this is the message you have heard from the beginning, that we should love one another, unlike Cain who belonged to the evil one and slaughtered his brother. Why did he slaughter him? Because his own works were evil, and those of his brother righteous.

1John 3:11-12

Evil is the Absence of Love

Evil is the absence of love. As bad as it can get, we know that evil dominate this world, which makes it a sad world, indeed. Negativity tugs at us and even grabs hold of us at times, but something else is continually pulls us toward the opposite, toward love. Just as darkness is the absence of light, evil is the absence of love. The absence of love is a proof of suffering; a person who does not love can't give loves, and thus suffer from not being love.

The spectrum of life is a spectrum of love, for God is love. On one end are pure love and the experience of oneness with all life, and on the other end are the absence of love and the experience of complete separation and evil. What exist in the absence of love is evil, and evil produce hateful acts. There are many people who have stored up love in their heart because of evil, and they are afraid to give that love or to share it. Fear can be a catalyst in which one doesn't give his love. This journey on earth, which takes many, many lifetimes, is a return to love and a rediscovery of our oneness. This is surely evidence that love is behind all life.

The fire is not a million sparks. It is just one fire. You cannot put it out one spark at a time. You must extinguish it all at once. This is how love and hate, good and evil work. The moment that you hold the works of the flesh, it implicates you in the cause of human suffering. Yes, we are a little implicated. Maybe you do not really know it yet, but now the seed have been planted, and the bitter fruit will grow. We are schooled to believe that we are all different, and that is where the seeds of hate are also sown. Our cultures are different, our expressions are different, but our experiences are all the same. We all suffer in many ways, we love, we struggle, we fear, we believe, we hope, we cling. Only where there is awareness of universal love is there an end to hate. Hate is just the absence of love just like jealousy is. Many people are full of hatred, anger, jealousy, they heart is full of bitterness because someone, somewhere, has rejected, belittled, diminished them. Now they have passed it unto you, like a great disease. You try to pass it on. You must develop a sense of love to really uproot the hate in you. You don't need to be a martyr. Love is in each and every one of us because we are made in God's image, and God is love. Love is more than simply an emotion; it is your essence.

The absence of love brings disaster, suffering in one's life and affects the environment you live in and the world. If you're not in a state of love you have conscious or unconscious fearful thoughts blocking your ability to have and be the love that is your true essence that leads to all kinds of negative feelings, including resentment, mistrust, and even hatred.

What is Evil?

Evil is usually thought of as that which is morally wrong, sinful, or wicked; however, the word evil can also refer to anything that causes harm, with or without the moral dimension. The word is used both ways in the Bible. Anything that contradicts the holy nature of God is evil. On the flip side, any disaster, tragedy, or calamity can also be called an "evil."

Evil, is the opposite of good, a profound wickedness who's taking multiple possible forms, such as the form of personal moral evil or impersonal natural evil, and in a religious thought, the form of the demonic or supernatural force. Evil denote a profound immorality and its definition vary, as does as the analysis of its motives. Evil deeds are:

Wicked, bad, wrong, immoral, sinful, ungodly, unholy, foul, base, ignoble, dishonorable, corrupt, iniquitous, depraved, degenerate, villainous, nefarious, sinister, vicious, malicious, malevolent, demonic, devilish, diabolic, fiendish, dark, black-hearted, monstrous, shocking, despicable, atrocious, heinous, odious, contemptible, horrible, execrable, egregious, flagitious, peccable and such as these. Evil behavior includes sin committed against other people (murder, theft, adultery) and evil committed against God (unbelief, idolatry, blasphemy). From the disobedience in the Garden of Eden (Gen 2:9) to the wickedness of Babylon the Great (Revelation 18:2), The Bible speaks of the fact of evil, and man is held responsible for the evil he commits. Essentially, evil is a lack of good. Moral evil is not a physical thing; it is a lack of privation of a good thing.

God is love, the absence of love in a person is un-God-like and therefore evil. And an absence of love manifests itself in unloving behavior. The same can be said concerning God's mercy, justice, patience, etc. the lack of these godly qualities in anyone constitutes evil. That evil then manifests itself in behavior that is unmerciful, unjust, impatient, immoral, etc. moral evil is wrong done to others, and it can exist even when unaccompanied by external action. Murder is an evil action, but it has its start with the moral evil of jealousy and hatred in the heart. Committing adultery is evil, but so is the moral evil of lust in the heart. It is from within, out of a person's heart that evil thoughts come-sexual immorality, theft, murder, adultery, greed, malice, deceit, lewdness, envies, slanders, arrogance, and folly. All these evils come from inside. Those who fall into evil and who practice evil are in Satan's trap and are slaves to sin. Physical evil is the trouble that befalls people in the world, and it may or may not be linked to moral evil or divine judgement. Sometimes, physical evil is simply the result of an accident or causes unknown, with no known moral cause; examples would includes injuries, car wrecks, hurricanes and earthquakes. Other times, physical evil is God's retribution for the sins of an individual or group. Sodom and the surrounding cities were destroyed for their sins (Genesis 19), and God "made them an example of what is going to happen to the evildoers and the ungodly. God is not the author of moral evil; rather, it is His holiness that defines it. Created in Good's image, we bear the responsibility to make moral choices that please God and conform to His will, which is our sanctification. God does not want or wish us to sin, and as God's children we walk according to this command: "Do not be overcome by evil, but overcome evil with good."

Light & Darkness

Light and darkness are constant themes. Those who live in darkness are confused, unable to see reality. Lost in the world of illusion they make judgments based on mere appearances, and are simply unable to grasp what is important and true. Light, on the other hand, cuts through this darkness to unveil the right and the true. And Jesus is the Cornerstone of the kingdom of light; we begin to "see" when we acknowledge Him as the Eternal Son of God. But "light" also has a moral dimension. And it is this moral dimension that Jesus affirmed as He not only presented Himself to Israel as God, but also claimed the right to establish a grace morality which is far higher than the legalistic morality of the Jews, for it alone truly reflects the morality of God.

Light and darkness represent good and bad, righteousness and evil, as well as truth and falsity. Christ, the Eternal Word is the One through whom righteousness has always been communicated. Christ planted a moral awareness deep in every person, and revealed the nature of goodness back. As the light of the world, Jesus reveals the morality of God. In Him we see beyond all previous revelations of the goodness. In His every action, Jesus gives a clear and unmistakable picture of grace. He shakes our old ideas of morality, and helps us to understand God's righteousness.

Light not only reveals that which is hidden in darkness, but it also provides energy needed for the giving and sustaining of life. God is light. When the earth was dark and void, God provided light. This light not only provided physical energy for the development of all life, including human beings, but it also provided spiritual direction, ultimately through the person of Jesus Christ, for the proper orientation of all life toward and in obedience to God's Word. Accordingly, the message that Jesus Christ brings to this world is one that will bring to light to the darkness of any heart. The whole world is dark, darkness covers the earth, and darkness is everywhere. "Darkness" refers to all that is opposed to God. This includes everything from the darkness of human sin to the dark power of Satan. God is not touched by sin, though He endured the sin of all mankind by allowing His Son Jesus Christ to die on the cross. From this we know that God has overcome sin though He Himself is not corrupted by sin. In this way, God's light is shed upon the darkness of all sin, allowing human beings the opportunity to escape the dark grip of sin for the light of God's love. We are assured of God's total supremacy over sin and its insidious corrupting nature. This is why (and how) "the Blood of Jesus purifies us from all sin," it is the Good News about the truth of God's love that is capable of overcoming any obstacle, no matter how dark.

Part Seven

THE PASSION OF THE CHRIST

For it is better to suffer for doing good, if that be the will of God, than for doing evil. For Christ also suffered for sins once, the righteous for the sake of the unrighteous, that He might lead you to God.

1Peter 3:17-18

A Man of Sorrows

B ehold, my servant shall deal prudently, he shall be exalted and extolled, and be very high. As many were astonied at thee; his visage was so marred more than any man, and his form more than the sons of men: so shall he sprinkle many nations; the kings shall shut their mouths at him: for that which had not been told them shall they see; and that which they had not heard shall they consider. Who hath believed our report? And to whom is the arm of the Lord revealed? For he shall grow up before him as a tender plant, and as a root out of a dry ground: he hath neither form nor comeliness; and when we shall see him, there is no beauty that we should desire him. He is despised and rejected of men; a man of sorrows, and acquainted with grief: and we hid as it were our faces from him; he was despised, and we esteemed him not. Surely he hath borne our griefs, and carried our sorrows: yet we did esteem him stricken, smitten of God, and afflicted. But he was wounded for our transgressions; he was bruised for our iniquities: the chastisement of our peace was upon him; and with his stripes we are healed.

All we like sheep have gone astray; we have turned every one to his own way; and the Lord hath laid on him the iniquity of us all. He was oppressed, and he was afflicted, yet he opened not his mouth: he is brought as a lamb to the slaughter, and as a sheep before her shearers is dumb, so he openeth not his mouth. He was taken from prison and from judgment: and who shall declare his generation? For he was cut off out of the land of the living: for the transgression of my people was he stricken. And he made his grave with the wicked and with the rich in his death; because he had done no violence, neither was any deceit in his mouth. Yet it pleased the Lord to bruise him; he hath put him to grief: when thou shalt make his soul an offering for sin, he shall see his seed, he shall prolong his days, and the pleasure of the Lord shall prosper in his hand. He shall see of the travail of his soul, and shall be satisfied: through his suffering, my righteous servant shall justify many, and their iniquities and guilt he shall bear. Therefore will divide him a portion among the great and he shall divide the spoil with the mighty; because he surrendered and hath poured out his soul unto death: and was counted among the wicked and numbered with the transgressors; and he bare the sin of many, and made intercession for the transgressors, and win pardon for their offenses. (Isaiah 52:13-54:1-12)

The Passion of the Christ

The life of Jesus Christ physically upon this earth was not necessarily a very pleasant existence. It is resumed in the words of the apostle St John in his gospel when he says "He came to His own, but his own people did not accept Him." (St John 1:11). There is nothing that can be as painful as heart-wrenching as to come into a community of people that should love and that should respect and should be expecting you and at the same time instead of love and a spirit of welcome, what you experienced is rejection. That rejection had nothing to do with anything that Jesus had done, but simply because Satan had so blinded the minds and the hearts of men that even God incarnated in human flesh coming into His own world was rejected.

Jesus was not really hated just for the things that He did and the things that He taught, but He was hated because of who He was. You have to understand that although man had that question about who Jesus was, Satan knew who Jesus was, and when Jesus got ready to cast out demons, there were occasions it was said to Him, "What have you to do with us, we know who you are, O Son of God?" Have you come here to torment us before the appointed time?" (St Matthew 8:29). Satan know that his time one day is going to run out, that's why he's doing everything that he can in order to confuse people, in order to messed up the minds of the people, he deceived mankind because he knows his time is soon be out.

You never seen such days, when there are so many efforts being made in order to make you doubt the deity of Jesus Christ. You got movies, you've got documentaries, you've got books, you've got professors lecturing and others talking about something they found in old books in ancient Egypt. You know the devil didn't started lying in modern days (John 8:44), he was a murderer from the beginning, and abode not in the truth, because there is no truth in him. When he lies, he speaks his native language, for he is a liar and the father of lies. The days when Jesus rose from the dead, when He came out of the tomb, when the soldiers who were there when He stepped out with all powers in His hands, the soldiers and guards ran into the city to tell those in authority above them that Jesus wasn't lying, because He has risen from the dead just as He said. Then the chief priests assembled with all the elders and took counsel; then they gave a large sum of money to the soldiers and told them to lies saying: "You are to say, 'His disciples came by night and stole Him while we were asleep. (St Matthew 28:11-15). The Da Vinci Code a movie completely designs to make you believe that Jesus was married to Mary Magdalene and that they had children. They've got all kinds of stuff going, trying to make you doubt who Jesus is.

Everyday Jesus was in the temple teaching, every evening He was spending the night in Bethany in the home of His friends Mary, Martha and Lazarus. Traps was set for Him, the Sadducees, the Herodian and the Pharisees trying to entangle Him because they determined from the time that He rode on a donkey to enter

Jerusalem, the people took palm branches and went out to meet Him, and cried out: "Hosanna! Blessed is He who comes in the name of the Lord, {even} the king of Israel. The Sadducees, the Herodian and the Pharisees came up with charges. They try a little bit of everything, they knew that Jesus was not like them but they also know that unless they got rid of Him that His teaching was going to overturn their lifestyle. So they set traps trying their very best to trap Him, but there was no way that they could even get to Him, until they found the traitor in His midst. So they got Judas Iscariot and a whole army going to a prayer meeting in order to captured one man. A whole army going to a garden where man's was praying in order to starts the wheel rolling to put him to death. Then they arrested Jesus, and then He had a trial at night. That was illegal because a legal trial had to take place in the day time.

Have you ever thought about your mission in life might be-not just what profession you might be like to work in but what your real purpose in life is? Maybe you haven't given it a lot of thought, but as you look toward graduation from high school and move on to work or more school or even volunteer service, it is something to which you will want to give some thought. Jesus had a clear understanding of his mission from an early age. And his mission will give you some clear direction about your purpose in life.

St Luke has a story about Jesus when He was twelve years old and became separated from His parents for three days (see St Luke 2:41-51). Mary and His foster father, Joseph, finally find Him talking with the Rabbis (Teachers) in the Temple in Jerusalem. When Mary begins to scold Jesus, He answers, "Did you not know that I must be in my Father's house?" (2:49). Then he returns with Mary and Joseph and is obedient to them. St Luke implies that even as a youngster, Jesus was aware of His special relationship to God and His mission.

Jesus' public life begins with His baptism by John the Baptist. Although Jesus had no need to be baptized because He was without sin (and John's baptism was about turning away from sin), He still asked John to baptize Him. In doing so Jesus identified Himself with sinners and anticipated the moment when He would take upon Himself the sin of all humankind. After His baptism, the Holy Spirit immediately took Jesus out into the desert to fast and pray and to be tested in preparation for His mission. During that time He rejected Lucifer's, the Devil's temptations to achieve His mission through fame, comfort, or political power. When Jesus returned from the desert, He was truly ready to begin His mission.

Each Gospel has its own variation on how Jesus announces His mission. For several years Jesus had been traveling in Galilee, Judea and Samaria, teaching, healing, and forming a band of disciples to continue His mission after His departure. Now His disciples were ready for the final challenge that lay ahead. One of them just announced that he believed Jesus to be the Messiah, the Son of the Living God. Then Jesus made the decision to travel to Jerusalem, where he would meet His death.

The Passion of Christ, from the Latin patior meaning "suffer," refers to those sufferings Jesus endured for our redemption from the agony in the garden of gethsemane until His death on Calvary. The Passion Narratives of the Gospels provide the details of our Lord's passion, and at least to some extent.

After the Last Supper, Jesus went to the Garden of Gethsemane at the Mount of Olives. Our Lord prayed, "Father, if it is your will, take this cup from me; yet not my will but yours be done" (St Luke 22:42). Jesus knew the sacrifice He faced. He prayed so intensely that "His sweat became like drops of blood falling to the ground" (St Luke 22:44). Our Lord was then arrested and tried before the Sanhedrin, presided over by the High priest Caiaphas. Responding to their questions, He proclaimed, "Soon you will see the Son of man seated at the right hand of the Power and coming on the clouds of heavens" (St Matthew 26:64). For this statement, Jesus was condemned to death for blasphemy, and was then spat upon, slapped, and mocked. While the Sanhedrin could condemn our Lord to death, it lacked the authority to execute; only Pontius Pilate, the Roman governor, could order an execution.

The Jewish leaders, therefore, took Jesus to Pilate; Pilate could not find conclusive evidence to condemn Jesus. Pilate challenged the chief priests, the ruling class, and the people, "I have examined Him in your presence and have no charge against Him arising from your allegations" (St Luke 23:14). When offering to release a prisoner, Pilate asked the crowd about Jesus: "What wrong is this man guilty of? I have not discovered anything about Him that calls for the death penalty?" (St Luke 23:22). Even Pilate's wife pleaded with him not to interfere in the case of "that holy man" (St Matthew 27:19). Pilate then had Jesus scourged (St John19:1). To enhance the scourging of our Lord, the soldiers added other tortures: crowing Him with thorns, dressing Him in a purple cloak, placing a reed in His right hand, spitting upon Him, and mocking Him, "All hail, king of the Jew!" (St Matthew 27:27-31).

After the scourging, Pilate again presented Christ to the crowd who chanted, "Crucify Him, crucify Him!" Fearing a revolt, Pilate capitulated and handed over Jesus to be crucified. The Romans had perfected crucifixion, which probably originated in Persia, to produce a slow death with the maximum amount of pain. Crucifixion was reserved for the worst criminals. This punishment was so awful that Cicero (43 BC) introduced legislation in the Roman Senate exempting Roman citizens from crucifixion; this is why St Paul was beheaded rather than crucified for being a Christian.

Jesus carried His own cross to further weaken Him. Since the entire cross weighed around 300 pounds, he usually carried only the horizontal beam (patibulum) weighing 75-125 pounds, to the place of execution where the vertical beams (stipes) were already in place. A military guard headed by a centurion led the procession. A soldier carried the titulus which displayed the victim's name and crime, and was later attached to the cross (St Matthew 27:37). For our Lord, the path from the praetorium to Golgotha was about 1/3 of a mile, and he was so weak Simon of Cyrene was forced to assist Him (St Matthew 27:32). Upon arriving at the place of execution, the law mandated the victim be given a bitter drink of wine mixed with myrrh (gall) as an analgesic (St Matthew 27:34). Jesus was then stripped of His garments, His hands were stretched over the patibulum and either tied, nailed or both. Archeological evidence reveals the nails were tapered iron spikes approximately seven inches in length with a square shaft about 3/8 of an inch. The nails were driven through the wrist between the radius and the ulna to support the weight of Jesus. The patibulum was affixed to the stipes, and the feet were then tied or nailed directly to it or to a small foot-rest (suppedaneum).

Jesus hung on the cross; the crowds commonly tormented Him with jeers. The soldiers divided His garments as part of their reward. As he hung in agony, insects would feed on the open wounds or the eyes, ears, nose, and birds in turn would prey on the victim. With the combined effects caused by the loss of blood, the trauma of scourging and dehydration, the weight of the body pulled down on the outstretched arms and shoulders impeding respiration, Jesus dies from a slow asphyxiation. Perhaps this is why Jesus spoke only tersely from the cross. If the person tried to life himself up on his feet to breath, incredible pain would be felt at the nail wounds and the back wounds from the scourging. To hasten death, the soldiers would break the legs of the victim. When Jesus appeared dead the soldiers insured the fact by piercing the heart with a lance or sword; when Jesus' heart was pierced, out flowed blood and water. Joseph of Arimathea asked Pilate for Christ's body, and he was then buried (St John 19:38).

The Passion of the Christ Explained

According to the Law of Moses regarding the Passover, the people of Israel were to select a lamb on the tenth day of the month. That lamb selected was to be kept until the fourteenth day where it would be slain in the evening. Jesus entered Jerusalem on Palm Sunday which was the tenth day of the month at that time. Therefore the fourteenth day was on Thursday. For the lamb selected the tenth was slain on the fourteen. On the fourteenth day the lamb was to be killed in the evening. St Mark tells us that Jesus was crucified on the third hour of the day at 9am, then at the sixth hour 12 noon, the sun blocked out, and in the ninth hour 3pm was when he died. So the Lamb was selected on the tenth was crucified first of all in the morning but it did not died until in the evening. For as the Lamb of God he has to measure up in every way. St John tells us that when Joseph of Arimathea went and begged Pilate for the body of Jesus, they did not want the body hanging on the cross on a Sabbath day because that day when he died was preparation so I found out that Israel had two kinds of Sabbath:

- There was the regular seven days of the week which we called Saturday
- There was also the high holy Sabbath that could occur any day in the week

But preceding a high holy Sabbath there had to be a preparation day, so Jesus died the day in front of the Sabbath, but he did not died the day before Saturday, He died the day before the high holy Sabbath which that year appeared on a Friday. When He rises, He rises at the end of the regular seventh day of the week. He rose following the seventh day of the week Sabbath, the regular Sabbath. But He died in front of a special holiday Sabbath which required a preparation day.

The Gospel writers do not tell us is that there were two Sabbaths which came together. He died in front of the holiday Sabbath which was Friday and he rose following the regular Sabbath which was Saturday. So if He died on the evening of Thursday, a part of Thursday He was in the grave, all night Thursday night, He was in the grave, all day Friday the holy Sabbath, He was in the grave, all night Friday night He was in the grave, all day Saturday the regular Sabbath, He was in the grave, all night Saturday night, He was in the grave, but early in the morning, after the Sabbath toward the dawn of the first day of the week, Jesus rose from the dead.

The Days of Jesus were filled with many struggles, filled with sufferings, filled with pain. I don't think that any human could ever imagine what it cost Jesus our Lord to leave the comfort of His abode in Heaven to come to this sin cursed earth. Jesus had every-thing, Archangels ready to answer His very best and His every call. Angels as servants, ready to minister His needs. Streets of gold, walls of jasper, gates of pearl, but He left everything that He has in Heaven and everything that He was in Heaven, for "He, being in the form of God, thought it not robbery to be equal with God:" But made Himself of no reputation, and took upon Him the form of a servant, and was made in the likeness of men, and being found in fashion as a man, He humbled himself and emptied Himself of His divinity and came down to be born on earth that the inn keeper didn't even have a room for Him, and so He had to be born in a stable, wrapped in swaddling clothes, lying in a manger.

Jesus lived the sinless life, He who did no sin, neither was guile found in His mouth, who, when He was reviled, reviled not again; when He suffered, He threatened not. He grew up a mid of accusing eyes of men and women who know that Mary had conceived Him before she and Joseph married. When He was trying to teach in the synagogues, some of those persons who did not understand who He was said: "Who are you? You're not even 40 years old and you're going to tell us something about our father Abraham."

Finally, they even went farther enough to say: "We are Abraham' seed and we were not born of fornication." This simply meant that they did not believe the story that Mary had conceived the child of the Holy Spirit. When He went back to His hometown, even after becoming a renowned evangelist, St Mark in chapter 6 says that "He could do there no mighty works because of their unbelief in Him." Finally, after chosen the 12 Disciples and given them power against unclean spirits and to cast demons and devils out, one of the 12 by the name of Judas Iscariot allowed Satan to fill his heart and sold Jesus His master for 30 pieces of silver. There is no way that we can tell the agony that Jesus suffered. He was spurned and rejected by men; a man of sorrows and suffering, accustomed with grief, one of those from whom men hide their faces, spurned, and we held him in no esteem.

Finally, that night in which He was betrayed, Judas Iscariot come leading a band of soldiers. Jesus had just finished the Passover with His Disciples, He had just finished taking the Cup saying: "This cup is the New Testament in My blood," He went out in the garden of gethsemane, there Judas leads a band of soldiers to arrest Him. As Jesus recognized what He has to go through, He is there praying and saying to the Father that "My soul is very sorrowful, even unto the death of the cross, and if there is another way, Father, if you're willing, let this cup pass over me but, nevertheless, not my will but as thou willing." And then He prayed more earnestly. He was oppressed, harshly treated; He submitted and opened not his mouth; like a lamb led to the slaughter or a sheep before the shearers, He was silent and opened not his mouth. Oppressed and condemned, He was taken away, and who would have thought any-more of His destiny? When He was cut off from the land of the living, and smitten for the sin of his people, a grave was assigned him among the wicked and a burial place with the evildoers, though He had done no wrong nor spoken any falsehood.

We cannot imagine what Jesus went through when Judas came and betrayed Him with a blistering kiss. And as the soldiers arrested Him, led Him away to Anna first then carried him into the direction of Caiaphas the high priest and his judgment hall. Most of Jesus' disciples fled, but Peter followed afar off. When they got to Caiaphas' courtroom, Peter sat over by the door warming Himself by the enemies fire, and a woman said: "he's one of them, Peter cursed and swear and said, "No, I don't know the man," but about that time, Jesus looked at him, reminding him that: I said, "before the cock shall crow, you're going to deny me three times." It was a very painful moment for Jesus. And that night Jesus was put to jail in custody. Early in the morning, Caiaphas took Jesus to Pilate; Pilate heard that Jesus was a Galilean and sends Him to Herod. Herod could not succeed in making Jesus perform a magic trick, so he sent Him back to Pilate. Pilate tried to get around the issue, saying "I'm not going to be guilty of this innocent man's blood, so give me a basin and let me wash my hands," the only thing I do is let you scourge Him, I let you give Him a good Roman beating, but I will not be guilty of putting him to death. They began to whip my Lord and savior, 39 lashes. If He had been beaten according to the Jewish law, it would have been 40 stripes save one. But it is said that the method of the Roman' flogging was that, they were beat one until he fail and then they would keep beating him until he look like he was within an inch of His life. The Romans used a short whip (flagrum or flagellum) with several single or braided leather thongs. Iron balls or hooks made of bones or shells were placed at various intervals along the thongs and at their ends. Cords, Cat o' Nine tails, that when they hit Him on His front and on His back, buttocks and legs. It would make an impression as they pulled the whip away; it would pull out little hunks of flesh. The scourging ripped the skin and tore into the underlying muscles, leaving the flesh into bloody ribbons. Jesus verged on circulatory shock and the blood loss would help determine how long He would survive

71

on the cross. To enhance the scourging of our Lord, the soldiers added other tortures: crowning him with thorns, dressing Him in a purple cloak, placing a reed in His right hand, spitting upon Him, and mocking Him. Jesus endured it all, not for any sins that He had done.

I wonder how could they do a man who was so good, How could they treat Him so bad? He was not guilty of insurrection, He was only guilty of performing all kinds of miracles, He was only guilty of opening blinded eyes, He was only guilty of unstopping deaf ears, He was only guilty of multiplying fish and loaves and feeding a hungry multitudes. Finally one day, they condemned him to death. He who did no sin, neither was guile found in His mouth, but they hanged Him on the cross. I ask the question, "Why are you allowing this to be done?" He said "Don't know man have the power to take my life from Me, I lay it down of Myself, that I might take it up again." And when I see Him with the crown of thorns on His head, nails in His hands, nails in His feet, a spear driven to His side, I want to know why are they doing this to Him? And I hear the voice of the prophet Isaiah ringing over 700 years of prophecy saying "Surely He hath borne our griefs, and carried our sorrow; yet we did esteem him stricken, smitten of God, and afflicted. But He was wounded for our transgressions; he was bruised for our iniquities: the chastisement of our peace was upon him; and with his stripes we are healed." (Isaiah 53:4-5). Jesus suffered and died because justice demanded that a penalty had to be paid, but it had to be paid by one without blemish and without spot. And when time was such that wasn't anybody else that could pay the price, St John on the isle of Patmos said a cry was made "Who is worthy to open the book, and to loose the seals thereof? (Revelation 5:2-8). A worldwide search was made, they went through the heavens and they couldn't find an angel that was worthy. They searched the earth and they couldn't find a man that was worthy, they went down to the sea and couldn't find one that was worthy, then they went down into the depths of hell and couldn't find one that was worthy, but after a while, as a lamb slain from the foundation of the world, he stepped down from under the altar and say" In burnt offerings and sacrifices for sin, thou hast had no pleasure, but a body thou hast prepared for Me, then I said, "Lo, I come to do thy will, O God." (Hebrews 10:5-8). Hanging on the cross between two thieves, bearing in his body the sins of mankind, inflicting on himself the worse suffering that could ever happened to him, Jesus offered up himself as the ultimate sacrifice to God by dying on the cross in order to bring redemption from sin, and a means back to God. As He looked in the Heavens and Heaven blocked out, but before it blocked out He saw the Father turned his back on him and he said: "Eli, Eli, lema Sabachthani"? That is, "My God, my God, why have you forsaken me?" (Mt 27:45-46). God had to turn his back on Jesus because when He looked on the cross He couldn't see Jesus, because He saw our sins, He saw our sicknesses and diseases hanging on Jesus and when He saw him covered with our sins God had to turn his back, but Jesus hanged out there on Calvary and He died all alone. Finally, when He said Father, into your hands I commend my spirit (John 23:46) because the body couldn't died as long as the spirit dwell within so He dismissed his spirit into the Throne Room of the Father. When He died, Joseph of Arimathea went to get his body, wrapped him up in linen clothes and he laid Jesus in his own new tomb and that spirit that Jesus commended to the Father while the body was reposed in sleep the spirit of Jesus went down in the spirits world, He went down into the deep recesses of hell to preach to those who were alive before the flood of Noah's time, Jesus held a revival back there and preach to the spirits that were in prison, men that Satan enslaved from the earliest time (1 Pt 3:18). And after His revival in hell, Jesus defeated hell, death, the grave and Satan, then He came out of the grave on Sunday Easter Morning in a glorify state and appeared to His disciples (Mary Magdalene, the two disciples on the Emmaus road, the ten disciples in the upper room...) and declared to them: "I am He that liveth, and was dead; and behold, I am alive for evermore. I have the keys of hell and death that I'm holding to my hands, All powers in heaven and earth has been given to me (Rev 1:17-18/ Mt 28:18). When He finished to talk to His disciples, He baptized them to receives the Holy Spirit (John 20:22) and He led them out to Bethany, lifted his hands and blessed them (Acts 1:4-11), and while He was blessing them, gravitation lost his hold, Jesus caught the nearest cloud and starting going up, He began to float, floated out into the Stratosphere, floated out pass the cloud, He kept rising until He got totally out of the Earth's Atmosphere, the Troposphere and the Arno sphere and sailed through in a Planetary space, passing by Jupiter, Saturn, Mars, Neptune, passing by the Moon, passing by the Stars, passing by the Sun and entered into the gates of the Father's Mansion, angels are kneeling; angels are veiling their faces and bowing before him. He sat down at the Right hand of the Throne of the Majesty on High and He looks at the Father and said: "Father, I told my church that when I got home, I'll send them another Comforter." And when Jesus went IN, the Holy Ghost came OUT, and early on Pentecost morning the Holy Ghost filled the house, the Holy Ghost got in the tongue of the disciples and they began to speak other languages and they went about all around to witness the Resurrection of the Christ (Acts 2:1-4/1:22).

In conclusion, I am glad that this is not the end of the story, when you read in the story books, the heroes always keep the glory for themselves, but Jesus, if you let me paraphrase it, He'll tell you: "I started it out in heaven, I didn't have to go through all that, I didn't have to leave the hallelujah of heaven, I didn't have to come down (and look how low He came?) He left heaven, somebody said that if he had stopped at the sun, it would have been a brighter world, if he had stopped at the moon, it would have been a center world, if he stopped at Jupiter, it would have been a mighty world, if he stopped at mercury, it would have been a faster moving world, by Saturn and other planets He was not seen, and mars had no man in which he could redeem but I'm glad that I can say to take my feet out of the miry clay, he came all the way down, down to poverty, down to being despised, down into the filth of this earth, down to be mingled with filthy sinners, down to be talked about, scandalized and spat on, and He went down into the earth and when He got up out of the grave, He didn't do anything but go back to where he started. He didn't have to do that for Himself, but He did it for you and me. He became sin that we could be righteous, He became poor that we could be rich, He died that we could live, and when he came up out of the grave, He had defeated our enemies but I heard St Paul saying in 1Corithians 15:57 But thanks be unto God who gives us the victory through our Lord Jesus Christ. He suffered it all for you; He suffered it all for me. He got up out of the grave to let us know that death is not the end of your life; he got up out of the grave to let us know that a called dirty grave is not our eternal home. And when he comes back, He's going to be like a thief and a robber by night, so he that is holy, let him be holy still, he that is righteous, let him be righteous still, he that is filthy, let him be filthy still. So when He comes back, I want to be caught up to meet Him in the air.

He Was Wounded for our Transgressions Explained

He is despised and rejected of men; a man of sorrows and suffering acquainted with grief: and we hid as it were our faces from him; He was despised, and we esteemed him not. Surely He hath borne our griefs, and carried our sorrows: Yet we did esteem Him stricken, smitten of God, and afflicted. But He was wounded for our transgressions; He was bruised for our iniquities: The chastisement that make us whole and of our peace was upon him; and with his stripes we are healed (Isaiah 53:3-5).

This prophecy of scripture from prophet Isaiah is from 700years before the coming of Jesus on earth and His passion. This passage, which focuses on the suffering of Jesus, unmistakably describes and explains the meaning of the death of Jesus Christ. It is one of the most vivid and important of all Old Testament prophetic passages. The wisdom of Jesus led him to make choices that seem foolish to men. He chose a path, obedience that led to intense and terrible suffering.

In Eden sin entered into the world through one Man Adam. In Gethsemane Jesus took upon himself the sin of the world including the sin of Adam. The night before they crucified Him, Jesus was led like a lamb to the slaughter, and as a sheep before her shearers is dumb. Jesus was severely scourged; they beat His front (torso) and His back. When they whipped him, it was really you and me that should have been getting the whipping (chastisement of our peace). Somebody said that if He was beaten after the methods of the Jews, 39 lashes were put on His back, but if He was beaten according to the custom of the Romans, He was just whipped with a Cat O' nine Tails, with little pieces of metal that when they hit His front and back and pulled it away that those little hunks of metal were pulled flesh from His bones. But He was beaten, His torso was beaten, His back was beaten in order to heal our back heads. I hope you understand what I'm saying, they took a crown of thorns, somebody said that there was 72 thorns that were plated, and a crown was put on His head, symbolizing anything that is happening in your head, it may be an ear trouble, it may be eyes trouble, it may be nose trouble, it may be tumor on your brain but they put a crown on His head in order to heal your headache. They nailed His hands that whatever is happening from the torso to the tips of your fingers may be healed. They nailed His feet, your swollen ankles, bunions, all kinds of stuff in your feet, all up to the knees down to the ankles, all the way up to the torso; whatever is going on, it was nailed to the cross in order that we may be healed. They took a spear and put it in His side and drove it up to his heart that anything that's happening in your torso, it does not matter if its stomach condition, kidney complaints, liver complaint, anything that's happening in your body... He was wounded for our transgressions; He was bruised for our iniquities: the chastisement of our peace was upon him; and with his stripes we are healed. (Isaiah 53:3-5).

Jesus' great act of self-sacrifice brought peace, healed, and lifted the sin-guilt from us. Jesus died a painful death. Therefore, we should not ignore the responsibility of the wicked men who plotted Jesus' death. But we must also realize that God Himself chose this course for Jesus. And Jesus freely elected to become a guilt offering, and thus be both priest and sacrifice. We are beneficiaries of Jesus' sacrificial act. We become His offspring, and because of Jesus take our place as children of God. We experience justification, and find in Jesus the freedom from the sins He bore in our place.

Part Eight

THE PARTICIPATION IN THE PASSION OF THE CHRIST

I have said these things to you, that in Me you may
have peace. In the world you will have tribulation.
But take heart; I have overcome the world.

St John 16:33

Causes of the Christian's Sufferings

The predicted suffering of the Christians is one of the major aspects of Christ prophecy concerning the future of His chosen people. It is paradoxical that the people chosen for exaltation and selected to be a special means of divine revelation namely the light of the world and the salt of the earth should also be destined for suffering which would exceed that of any other religion of the world.

The temptations, trials, tests, tribulations, persecutions and sufferings of the Christians stem from the basic conflict between divine purpose and satanic opposition. The very fact that God so loved the world and gave His only Son, so that everyone who believes in Him might not perish but might have eternal life (St John 3:16) makes the chosen and selected people, the Believers-Christians , the object of special satanic attack. Satan hatred of the seed of the woman particularly the seed of God through Jesus Christ is manifested from the beginning culminating in the rebellion at the end of the millennium.

Spiritual warfare in relation to the Christians is in evidence from the beginning at the birth of Jesus. The corrupting influence of Satan is manifest, Herod ordered the massacre of all the boys in Bethlehem and its vicinity two years old and under (St Matthew 2:16-18), and only by the grace of God was Jesus sent to go to Egypt He and Joseph and Mary His mother. Through King Herod, Satan sought to spoil, to hinder, to obstruct and to mar the purpose of God in Jesus and the elect nation Israel. The scattering of Israel in the captivities, the attempt recorded in the Book of Esther to

exterminate the Jew, and the ultimate capstone of satanic opposition to Israel's place of spiritual leadership was recorded in the
gospels. Israel's rejection of her Messiah is related, with Israel's
resulting dispersion following the Roman persecution A.D. 70-135.
Undoubtedly one of the principal causes for Israel's suffering and
the Christians have been the unending opposition of Satan to the
fulfillment of God's purpose in the nation.

Satan hates God; he has a deep hatred toward God and God's
people. As I ponder this reality and this fact, I see more and more
evidence to support the statement used as a title for this. Sure, there
is the obvious logical agreement: Satan hates God, and since Satan
is called the god of this world and we know that the whole world
lies under the power of Satan. Therefore, seeing the work of Satan
in our secular society, the idea of God is twisted into a perversion
and caricature of reality and the convicting work of the Holy Spirit
is undermined by persistent indoctrination in the lie of autonomy
and guiltless existence. The day you put your faith in Jesus Christ,
your eternal address changed from a place known as hell to a place
called heaven. It was a day in which you passed from darkness to
light, a day in which you found new purpose and meaning. It was
also a day in which a very real spiritual war began in your life.
Conversion made your mind and hearts a battlefield. You came to
realize that not only is there a God who loves you, but there is also
a devil who hates you and wants to pull you back into your old
ways again where he got you the first time.

Christians are the special object of satanic hatred in this world.
This is borne out in the prophecy concerning the woman with child
in Revelation 12. The best explanation of this symbolic presentation
is that the woman is Israel/the Church and the child is Lord Jesus
Christ. The dragon, representing Satan, is portrayed as being cast
down to the earth in Revelation 12:13 and, realizing that his time
is short, according to the Scripture, "he persecuted the woman that
brought forth the man child" (Revelation 12:13). The Scriptures

which follow indicate the unrelenting warfare against the woman and her seed and only by divine intervention is partial protection afforded her. Therefore, the sufferings of the Christians should be seen in the context of satanic persecution, of divine discipline for sin, and of divine faithfulness to His chosen people.

The important world events which are taking place today may be regarded as a prelude to the consummation which will include Israel's time of suffering. Heart-rending as it may be to contemplate, the people of Israel who are returning to their ancient land are placing themselves within the vortex of this future whirlwind which will destroy the majority of those living in the land of Palestine. The searching and refining fire of divine judgment will produce in Israel that which is not there now, an attitude of true repentance and eager anticipation of the coming of their messiah. The tribulation period will then be followed by Israel's day of glory.

For the Christian these events are of utmost significance, Christ will come for His church, the body of saints, in this present age of grace, before these end-time event take place namely: "The Tribulation of the church of Jesus Christ and the Great tribulation of Israel." The swiftly moving events of our generation are not a basis for despair, but another reminder that God majestically fulfill His will. Every prophecy will find its counterpart in complete fulfillment, and the wisdom and mercy and sovereignty of God will be vindicated before all His creatures. Christ is not only the hope of the Christians but also the hope of Israel and of all those who are trusting Him.

The Participation in the Passion of Christ

Partakers of Christ's Sufferings

Beloved, do not be surprised concerning the fiery trial that is occurring among you and which is to try you, as though some strange thing were happening to you. But rejoice to the extent that you share in the sufferings of Christ, so that when His glory is revealed, you may be glad also with exceeding joy. (1Peter 4:12-13).

What does it mean to participate in the passion of the Christ?

It simply means that a person is aware of what Christ has suffered and has done for him/her; that person freely and willingly accepts to share in the same sufferings of Christ. Jesus Christ suffered because of us; He suffered because of you and me. He didn't suffer for Himself and because Christ suffered, I must be partakers of Christ's sufferings. It is just saying "I am suffering because Christ suffered for me". When you receive Jesus Christ as your Lord and Savior, there is a price to pay. The sufferings of Christ were not those of ordinary people. He suffered for our sake "according to the will of God," having a different point of view of suffering from ours.

The participation in the passion of the Christ is the consequence sufferings, meaning that Jesus Christ is the consequence of why I am experiencing this suffering. It is the kind of suffering that occurs in our lives to make us see, feel, experience and understand partially what Christ suffered and experienced because of us. This kind of suffering helps us understand what takes place in the suffering in the life of Christ. Because of this process, you will never be surprised by what comes your way.

Ways Christ' Suffered

Jesus' sufferings were more than just physical. The Lord experienced the full range of human suffering, to the greatest extent:

He put upon Himself a human body: *"Let this mind be in you, which was also in Christ Jesus, who being in the form of God, did not regard equality with God something to be grasped. Rather, He made Himself of no reputation, He emptied Himself, taking the form of a slave servant, being born in the likeness of man, coming in human likeness, and being found human in appearance,*

He humbled Himself and become obedient unto death, even death on the cross" (Philippians 2:5-8).

He was born in a stable: *"And she brought forth her first-born son, and wrapped Him in swaddling clothes, and laid Him in a manger; because there was no room for them in the inn"* (St Luke 2:7).

He was persecuted to death as a child: *"And when they were departed, behold, the angel of the Lord appeared to Joseph in a dream, saying, Arise, and take the young child and His mother, and flee to Egypt, and stay there until I tell you. Herod is going to search for the child to destroy Him"* (St Matthew 2:13).

He and His parents lived in fear as a child: *"But when he heard that Archelaus was ruling over Judea in place of his father Herod, he was afraid to go back there. And because he had been warned in a dream, he departed to the district of Galilee"* (St Matthew 2:22)

He grew up a mid of accusing eyes of men and women who know that Mary had conceived Him before she and Joseph married: *"Then said they to Him, we are not illegitimate. We were not born of fornication, of sexual immorality"* (St John 8:41).

He was rejected: *He came to His own but His own people did not accept Him.* (St John 1:11)

He was homesick: *"Jesus answered, My kingdom is not of this world, if my kingdom were of this world, my servants would have been fighting, that I might not be delivered over to the Jews. But my kingdom is not from this world"* (St John 18:36).

He was tempted and tested: *"Being forty days tempted of the devil. And in those days He did eat nothing; and when they were ended, he afterward hungered"* (St Luke 4:2).

He was discriminated and judged: *"Then answered the Jews, and said unto Him, Are we not right in saying that you are a Samaritan, and are demonically possessed?* (St John 8:48).

His soul was sorrowful: *"Then he said unto them, My soul is very sorrowful, even to death"* (St Matthew 26:38).

He was homeless: *"And Jesus said to him, Foxes have holes, and birds of the air have nests, but the Son of man has nowhere to lay His head"* (St Matthew 8:20).

He was hated by the world: *"If the world hates you, ye know that it hated Me before it hated you"* (St John 15:18).

He was oppressed and persecuted: *"So from that day on they made plans to put Him to death"* (St John 11:52-53).

He was betrayed by His own: *"Judas, would you betray the Son of man with a kiss?* (St Luke 22:48).

He was in agony because He carried the burden of the sins of the world: *"And being in agony He prayed more earnestly and his sweat was as it were great drops of blood falling down to the ground"* (St Luke 22:44).

He was taken captive: *"Then they came up and laid hands on Jesus and seized him"* (St Matthew 26:50).

He was deserted, abandoned by His own: *"Then all the disciples left Him and fled"* (St Matthew 26:56).

He was denied by His own: *"Peter said I am not His disciple"* (St John 18:17-18).

He was falsely accused and rejected by Jewish leaders and by those in the crowd: *"Now the chief priests, and elders, and all the council, sought false witness against Jesus, to put Him to death; but found none, yea, though many false witnesses came, yet they found nothing"* (St Matthew 26:59-60/26:67-68).

He was unfairly held in Custody: *"Now the men who were holding Jesus in custody were mocking Him as they beat Him"* (St Luke 22:63)

He was rejected by men not because of anything He has done: *"The governor again said to them, which of the two do you want me to release for you? And they said, 'Barabbas' Pilate said* *to them, then what shall I do with Jesus who is called Christ? They all said, Let Him be crucified"* (St Matthew 27:21-22).

He was scourged not for what he has done: "Then he released for them Barabbas, and having scourged Jesus, delivered him to be crucified" (St Matthew 27:26).

He was spat upon and beat up for tour sins: *"Then they spit in His face and struck Him. And some slapped him, saying 'Prophesy to us, you Christ! Who is it that struck you"?* (St Matthew 26:67-68).

He was humiliated for our sake: *"And they stripped Him, and put on him a scarlet robe"* (St Matthew 27:28/26:67-68)

He was pressed with a sharp crown of thorns that penetrated his brow, skull, even to His brain because of us: *"And when they had platted a crown of thorns, they put it upon His head, and a reed in His right hand, and they bowed the knee before him, and mocked him"* (St Matthew 27:29).

He was mocked and abused for telling the truth: *"And kneeling before him, they mocked Him, 'Hail, King of the Jews! And they spit on Him and took the reed and struck Him on the head"* (St Matthew 27:29-30).

He was reviled, derived and despised by men: *"And those who passed by reviled Him, waging their heads"* (St Matthew 27:39-41).

He was nailed to the cross from the third hour till the ninth hour (9am to 3pm): *"And it was the third hour, and they crucified Him"* (St Mark 15:25-33)

He was crucified between two thieves: *The thieves also, which were crucified with Him also reviled Him in the same way"* (St Mark 15:27/St Matthew 27:44).

His body was pierced with a spear: *"But one of the soldiers with a spear pierced His side, and forthwith came there out blood and water"* (St John 19:34).

He died: *"And Jesus cried out again with a loud voice and yielded up His ghost"* (St Matthew 27:50).

He tasted death for all. This is the most horrible reality of the cross. Christ did not die metaphorically or symbolically. He died literally. The Son of God, who had never sinned and who was least deserving death died so we could have life. His heart stopped beating, He stopped breathing and His spirit left His body. Love but not loved. Possibly the greatest interior agony Jesus was the hard and cruel fact of his mission of love being rejected. Jesus gives freedom to every individual on earth. Therefore, he forces himself on nobody. His love not being accepted, especially His love manifested by His suffering, caused Jesus mortal anguish.

Suffering for Christ's Sake

The suffering for Christ's sake simply mean that a person is already sell out to Christ, aware of what Christ has done, decided to make up his mind that anything and everything that happens to me is for Christ. Christ is the cause, not suffering as a murderer, not as a thief, not as an evildoer, or as an intriguer but suffering for Christ. I am suffering for Him. This suffering for Christ can be manifested in two-fold way sufferings:

Suffering the Loss of all things for the sake of Christ

Suffering for the Name of Jesus

I. Suffering the Loss of All Things for the Sake of Christ.

But whatever gain I have those I counted as loss for the sake of Christ. Yea doubtless, more than that, I even consider everything as a loss because of the supreme good of knowing Christ Jesus my Lord. For His sake I have suffer the loss of all things and consider them so much rubbish, in order that I may gain Christ and be found in Him, not having any righteousness on my own based on the law but that which comes through faith in Christ, the righteousness from God that depends on faith. That I may know Him, and the power of His resurrection, and the fellowship of His sufferings, being made conformable unto His death. (Philippians 3:7-11).

What does it mean to count everything as loss for the sake of Christ? What does it mean to renounce all that we have for Christ's sake?

In everyday, practical terms, what does it mean to do this? It means renouncing all, that is renouncing Me, Myself and I, the world and everything this world has to offer (the love of this world, the pride of possessions, the lust of the flesh, the lust of the eyes and the pride of life). I renounce all of these things. It means everything I have in this world, all the material good and possessions, fame, popularity, riches, wealth; I renounce all of that to follow Christ. It's an act of faith but the good news is when I do that, Christ give it back to me another way. I am no longer the center of my life, all my needs all my desires are now turn toward Christ's need and desires. Christ is first and foremost. If I must choose between Christ and anything else, I will choose Christ. That, is even though God does not bring me to the crisis of either-or at every point, nevertheless, I am ready, and have resolved in my heart that, if the choice must be made, I will choose Christ.

Renouncing all means also that I will seek to deal with the things of this world in ways that show that they are not my treasure, but rather that Christ is my treasure. That is, I will hold things loosely, share things generously, and ascribe value to things in relation to Christ. I will seek to live the paradox of 1 Corinthians 7:30-31: "And they that weep, as though they wept not; and they that rejoice, as though they rejoiced not; and they that buy, as though they possessed not; and those who deal with the world as though they had no dealings with it. For the present form of this world is passing away".

Renouncing all means that I will deal with everything in ways that draw me nearer to Christ, so that I gain more of Christ, and enjoy more of Him, by the way I relate to everything. That is, I will embrace everything pleasant by being thankful to Christ, and I will endure everything hurtful by being patient through Christ.

Renouncing all means that if I lose any or all the things this world can offer, I will not lose my joy, or my treasure, or my life because Christ is my joy and my treasure and my life. That is, in smaller losses I will not grumble (Philippians 2:14), and in greater losses I will grieve, but not as those who have no hope (1 Thessalonians 4:13). Jesus said to all, "If anyone would come after me, let him deny himself and take up his cross daily and follow me. For whoever would save his life will lose it, but whoever loses his life for my sake will find it and save it. (St Luke 9:-23-24/St Matthew 16:24-25). Then Peter began to say unto Him, "See, we have left everything and have followed you." Jesus answered and said, "Truly I say unto you, there is no man who has left house or brothers or sisters or mother or father or children or lands, for my sake and for the gospel, who will not receive a hundredfold now in this time, houses and brothers and sisters and mothers and children and lands, with persecutions, and in the age to come eternal life. (St Mark 10:28-30).

This is what I believe it means to find Jesus so all-sufficient and all-satisfying that (1) we count everything as loss (Philippians 3:8), (2) renounce all our possessions (St Luke 14:33), and, (3) "sell" all we have to possess the treasure of the person of Christ (St Matthew 13:44). None of us loves Christ this perfectly, or lives so consistently. But to be a follower of Jesus, to be a true Christian, means that these ways of dealing with "everything" will be the settled, joyful, defining resolve of our lives. This is what I believe it means to find Jesus so all-sufficient and all-satisfying that we can say with St Paul, "I count everything as loss because of the surpassing worth of knowing Christ Jesus my Lord."

II. Suffering for the Name of Jesus. (Acts 5:41)

And they departed from the presence of the council, rejoicing that they were counted worthy to suffer shame for the Name of Jesus (Acts 5:41).

The Name of Jesus Explained

"Now the birth of Jesus Christ took place in this way. When as His mother Mary was espoused to Joseph, before they came together, she was found with child of the Holy Spirit. Then Joseph her husband, being a just man, and not willing to put her to shame and make her a public example, was minded to put her away privily, resolved to divorce her quietly. But while he thought on these things, behold, the angel of the Lord appeared unto him in a dream, saying, Joseph, thou son of David, fear not to take unto you Mary as your wife, for that which is conceived in her is from the Holy Spirit. And she will bring forth a son, and you shall call His NAME JESUS: for He shall save His people from their sins". (St Matthew 1:18-21).

We're living in a world now particularly in the united States and the western hemisphere, I think about the African-American, I think about the portion of this world that in early days were not really exposed to so many of the other religions of the East. Eastern culture has come our way and with it so many different religions and different attitudes and different customs and different traditions, but one thing we must remember is that Jesus Christ is either Lord of all or else He is not Lord at all. The Word of God has not point us into many directions or into many roads. And yet there are some who believe that if you live in one part of the world, you can be saved by at hearing to one ideology, one religion, and one concept. And if you live in another part of the world then you can make it to heaven by following another road. But when we read the Bible and what the Word of God has say to us, even the prophet Isaiah who lived in the day's maybe about 700 years prior to the birth of

Jesus. He saw that the plan of God that was busily unfolding was come to its completion, its fulfillment with the birth of Jesus Christ. Once Jesus comes on the scene, the angel announced to Joseph who was thinking about Mary having an abortion, in other words, here Mary was pregnant with child, he knew she was his espoused wife, it had not being consummated but she had just came back from a three months' vacation visiting Elizabeth in the hill country. And when she came back, she had all the evidences of being with child, and Joseph was thinking about putting her away by writing a bill of divorcement or putting her away by stoning her to death, since in Israel, adultery means also stoning to death. So while Joseph is ponding in his heart, in his mind, how am I going to do this without making a public spectacle out of Mary? The angel of the Lord appeared to him and spoke to him (St Matthew 1:19-20). Jesus was named prophetically, and His name was given by an angel from Heaven. Our salvation was not purchased by the babe of Bethlehem but by the man who Jesus became, for redemption was not child play, but redeeming us from sin was a man' size job.

What is in the name? It all depends on what the name is. We live in a society where we understand that certain names will unlock doors. The Lord said to Abram "Go forth from the land of your kinsfolk and from your father's house to a land that I will show you (Genesis 12:1-3). God promised Abram seven blessings, and among those seven things that God said to Abram that he would do, in the midst of everything else that God promised to Abram that he would do, He said to him: "I will make your name great." And there is something about it God has a way of even making some names great that while you call on one name and people pay you no attention, then you can call another name and people would stop whatever they're doing because that name has power in a partic- ular circle. Well, what we have to recognize is that as we live upon this earth, we are human creatures, we live in the body of flesh but sometimes we put too much emphasis on that which you see, that which you see the body is not so important, it is really the spirit man that dwells inside of the body. When you try to get someone to do something, you are looking at their body but it's their mind you're trying to change, it is that invisible, that intangible part that you want to get to in order to make the body act right. And all of us as human creatures we are susceptible to two great spiritual powers, either it is the power of God, the power of good from above or it is the power of evil from beneath, and when you are having trouble with the power of evil from beneath, whether you call him Satan, the devil, the evil spirit, I don't care what you call him, there is one name that will make him behave, the only name that you can call that would cause demons to trembled, the only name that you can call that would make even Satan himself the chief evil spirit back up stand back and take notice. You can call your name all you want to, you can call you daddy name and nothing happens, you can even call the name of some who even call themselves savior of such, you may call the name of Buddha, you may call the name of Mohammed or you may call the name of Confucius, you may call the name of Zoroaster, I don't care how many names you call, you can go back and get the Egyptians gods and call their names, but there is NO NAME that would make hell take notice unless you call the Name of Jesus. Acts 4:11-12 says, This Jesus is the stone that was rejected by you, the builders, which has become the cornerstone. And there is salvation in no one else, for there is no other name under heaven given among men by which we must be saved. And in the book of Philippians 2:9 it is written, Therefore God has highly exalted Him and giving Him a name that is above every name, so that at the name of Jesus every knee should bow, in heaven and on earth and under the earth, and every tongue confess that Jesus Christ is Lord, to the Glory of God the Father.

There are things that bothered the people of the world, especially the Christian's haters, the atheist and other religious organizations. One thing is the name of Jesus that really got under their skin. In the days of Jesus and the Apostles, the Jewish leaders were bothered that the preaching of the Apostles and the miracles being performed were in the name of Jesus of Nazareth, whom they had crucified. The way they speak of "that name" again and again shows how disturbed they were by it. From their point of view, Jesus was only an upstart teacher and He had come from who knows where and had taken it upon Himself to be a rabbi. There was something behind their opposition. Jealousy had been festering within them. Even today, many people today are still bothered by the name of Jesus, they don't want to hear it and as one confess the name and preach it, he must expect persecution and suffering because of the name.

Suffering to serves as a Way to be like Christ

Remember the word that I said to you: 'A servant is not greater than his master.' If they persecuted Me, they will also persecute you. If they kept My word, they will also keep yours." (St John 15:20).

To be like Christ will take you to a process of pruning, a process of suffering; for every branch of Jesus that does bear fruit, God prunes it. And the process of pruning is the process of suffering and this process will serve as a way to be like Christ.

The Person of Christ: His Nature

Jesus is love, Jesus is true, Jesus is good, Jesus is faithful, Jesus is merciful, Jesus is kind, Jesus is gracious, Jesus is patient, Jesus is righteous, Jesus is just, Jesus is compassionate, Jesus is peace, Jesus is holy, Jesus is powerful, Jesus is meek, Jesus is humble, Jesus is wise, Jesus is forgiveness, Jesus is all knowing, Jesus was a servant, Jesus was a healer, Jesus was a teacher, Jesus was a preacher, etc.

Becoming like Christ is the desire of every believer, and it is encouraging to know that God has the same desire for us. In fact, the Bible says that God "predestined us to be conformed to the likeness of his Son (Romans 8:29). Making us Christ' like is God's work, and He will see it through to the end (Philippians 1:6). However, the fact that God will transform us into the image of Christ doesn't mean we can sit back and be carried to heaven "on flow'ry beds of ease." The process demands our willing cooperation with the Holy Spirit because becoming like Christ requires both divine power and the fulfillment of human responsibility.

The ultimate goal of every Christian is to look like Jesus; it is to follow Jesus in both the big and small areas of our lives, in order to be the blessing that He was on earth, and to receive the blessings of obedience to and pursuit of God. This is what we all want, but so few of us feel we are progressing at the place we'd prefer.

Suffering to be counted as a Legitimate Son of God

For consider Him who has endured such hostility by sinners against himself, so that you may not grow weary and lose heart. You have not yet resisted to the point of shedding blood in your striving against sin; and you have forgotten the exhortation which is addressed to you as sons, "My son, do not regard lightly the discipline of the Lord, nor faint when you are reproved by Him; for those whom the Lord loves he disciplines, and he scourges every son whom He receive." It is for discipline that you endure: God deals with you as with sons; for what son is there whom his father does not discipline?...All discipline for the moment seems not to be joyful, but sorrowful; yet to those who have been trained by it, afterwards it yields the peaceful fruit of righteousness. (Hebrews 12:3-11).

The Discipline of God & the Testing of our Faith.

Consider it all joy, my brothers, when you encounter various trials, for you know that the testing of your faith produces perseverance. And let perseverance be perfect, so that you may be perfect and complete, lacking in nothing (James 1:1-4).

95

Through this kind of suffering and hardship, God is disciplining us; He is teaching us and correcting us and transforming us. In other words, God has a purpose and a design in what is happening to us. God is the ultimate doer here. God is not passive observer in our lives while sinners and Satan beat us up. He rules over sinners and Satan, and they unwittingly, and with no less fault or guilt, fulfill His wise and loving purposes of discipline in our lives (Job 1-2). In this kind of suffering, God is the doctor planning our surgery. This is the design of our loving Father that comes to us painfully and mysteriously through the hostility of sinful adversaries and the natural hazards of a fallen world. If we submit to His sovereign, loving, Fatherly care, we will not "grow weary and lose heart," but we will keep the faith, fight the good fight, and finish our course, and die well, and glorify our Father in Heaven.

Suffering as a Christian

We are troubled on every side, yet not distressed; we are perplexed, but not in despair; persecuted, but not forsaken; cast down, but not destroyed; always bearing about in the body the dying of the Lord Jesus, that the life also of Jesus might be made manifest in our body (2Corinthians 4:8-10). For I reckon that the sufferings of this present time are not worthy to be compared with the glory which shall be revealed in us (Romans 8:18).

For followers of Jesus, the Christians, the picture of suffering is more sobering. The Bible promises us persecution and suffering for our faith. The whole world is in rebellion against God. It hates God, and when God came as a man in the person of Jesus Christ, the world responded by murdering Him. Jesus foretold us that the world would treat us the way it treated Him (John 15:20).

The first followers of Jesus consistently experienced suffering for the sake of Jesus, in Jerusalem (Acts 8:1), Galatia (Gal. 3:4), Philippi (Philippians 1:29), Thessalonica (1Thessalonians 2:14), and Asia Minor (1 Peter 4:12), along with the recipients of the letter to the Hebrews (Hebrews 10:32). St Paul went through horrible suffering (2Corinthians 11:23-29), as did the other apostles (Acts 5-8).

Persecution, opposition and suffering are a normal part of the normal Christian life. The comfortable experience of Christians in the West has actually been an anomaly in this regard. Because the Christian heritage of Western civilization, combined with democratic freedoms and historic rule of law, Western Christians have largely been left alone for their faith. Even today, as Western nations become increasingly post-Christian (and even anti-Christian), the opposition experienced by most Christians goes little beyond mockery. However, there are signs that this protected status may be changing. If it continues to do so, it will simply put Western Christians in the same boat as their brothers and sisters all over the world.

Today, in Islamic, Hindu, and Communist parts of the world, being a follower of Jesus means, at best, losing your job and being rejected by your family. At worst, it can mean imprisonment, beating, and even death. These things are being experienced all over the world right now by our brothers and sisters in Jesus. And as followers of Jesus, we do not rejoice in suffering because we enjoy pain, but because Jesus is so worthy in our eyes and hearts that we delight in being identified with Him. We should not be surprised or caught off guard by suffering. We are called to endure suffering and thus we need to endure suffering without compromising our integrity. We must love our persecutors and pray for their welfare and renouncing any intention to take revenge. We are to trust God in the midst of our suffering and respond by proactively doing good. We are to use our experiences of suffering as a basis for comforting others who suffer, telling them to fix their eyes on Jesus, and commanding them to rejoice. All suffering is temporary. It isn't worth comparing with the glory that awaits us.

In that place of glory, all pain and suffering will be gone forever (Revelation 21:4).

Suffering to Enter the Kingdom of God

After they had proclaimed the good news to that city and made a considerable number of disciples, they returned to Lystra and to Iconium and to Antioch. They strengthened the spirits of the disciples and exhorted them to persevere in the faith, saying, "It is necessary for us to undergo many hardships to enter the kingdom of God" (Acts 14:21-22).

Christianity and the Christian' life is about endurance and perseverance of faith, as we walk toward God's eternal kingdom, along the path that passes "through much tribulation." Jesus Christ declared that His way is "difficult" and His gate "narrow" (St Matthew 7:14). God allows Christians to have trials and serious problems even though we are striving to obey and please Him.

There is vital quality that God desires in all humans before He allows them to enter His kingdom. This super important quality is to build the character of Christ in us (obedience, holiness, righteousness, truth, trust in God, faith, sanctification, love, kindness, humility, faithfulness, long-suffering, patience, joy, peace, gentleness, goodness, meekness, temperance...). This kind of character must be developed in each Christian before he or she can receive the reward of eternal life in the kingdom of God. God will make those who are to enter His kingdom fully like His Son Jesus Christ! St John is explicit: "Behold what manner of love the father has bestowed upon us, that we should be called the children of God!... Beloved, now we are the children of God; and it does not yet appear what we shall be, but we know that when He shall appear, we shall be like Him, and we shall see Him as He is (1John 3:1-3). This is the awesome potential of all who receive eternal life as members of the family God is creating!

Love One Another

Now this is the message that we have heard from Him and proclaim to you: God is light, and in Him there is no darkness at all. If we say, "We have fellowship with Him," while we continue to walk in darkness, we lie and do not act in truth. But if we walk in the light as he is in the light, then we have fellowship with one another, and the blood of Jesus His Son cleanses us from all sin. If we say, "we are without sin," we deceive ourselves, and the truth is not in us. If we acknowledge our sins, He is faithful and just and will forgive our sins and cleanse us from every wrongdoing. If we say, "we have not sinned," we make Him a liar, and His word is not in us. But if anyone does sin, we have an advocate with the Father, Jesus Christ the Righteous One. He is expiation for our sins and not for us only but for those of the whole world. The way we may be sure that we know Him is to keep His commandments. Whoever says: "I know Him," but does not keep His commandments is a liar and the truth is not in him. But whoever keeps His word, the love of God is truly perfected in him. This is the way we may know that we are in union with Him. Whoever claim to abide in Him ought to live [just] as he lived. Whoever says he is in the light, yet hates his brother, is still in the darkness. Whoever loves his brother remains in the light, and there is nothing in him to cause a fall. Whoever hates his brother is in darkness; he walks in darkness and does not know where he is going because the darkness has blinded his eyes. And now, children, remain in Him, so that when He appears we have confidence and not be put to shame by Him at His coming. If you consider that He is righteous, you also know that everyone who acts in righteousness is begotten by Him.

See what manner of love the Father has bestowed upon us that we may be called the children of God. Yet so we are. The reason the world does not know us is that it did not know Him. Beloved, we are God's children now; what we shall be has not yet been revealed.

We do know that when it is revealed we shall be like Him, for we shall see Him as He is. Everyone who has this hope based on Him makes himself pure, as he is pure. Everyone who commits sin commits lawlessness, for sin is lawlessness. You know that He was revealed to take away sins, and in Him there is no sin. No one who remains in Him sins; no one who sins has seen Him or known Him. Children, let no one deceive you. The person who acts in righteousness is righteous, just as He is righteous. Whoever sins belongs to the devil, because the devil has sinned from the beginning. Indeed, for this cause the purpose of the Son was manifested to destroy the works of the devil. No one who is begotten by God commits sin, because God's seed remains in him; he cannot sin because he is begotten by God. In this way, the children of God and the children of the devil are made plain; no one who fails to act in righteousness belongs to God, nor anyone who does not love his brother.

For this is the message: we should love one another, unlike Cain who belonged to the evil one and slaughtered his brother. Why did he slaughter him? Because his own works were evil, and those of his brother righteous. Do not be amazed, [then,] brothers, if the world hates you. We know that we have passed from death to life because we love our brothers. Whoever does not love remains in death. everyone who hates his brother is a murderer, and you know that no murderer has eternal life remaining in him. The way we came to know love was that Jesus Christ laid down His life for us; so we ought to lay down our lives for our brothers. If someone who has worldly means sees a brother in need and refuses him compassion, how can the love of God remain in him? Children, let us love not in word or speech but in deed and truth.

[Now] this is how we shall know that we belong to the truth and reassure our hearts before Him in whatever our hearts condemn, for God is greater than our hearts and knows everything. Beloved, if [our] hearts do not condemn us, we have confidence in God and receive from Him whatever we ask, because we keep His commandments and do what pleases Him. And His commandment is this: we should believe in the name of His Son, Jesus Christ, and love one another just as He commanded us. Those who keep His commandments remain in Him, and He in them, and the way we know that He remains in us is from the Spirit He gave us.

Beloved, do not trust every spirit but test the spirits to see whether they belong to God, because many false prophets have gone out into the world. This is how you can know the Spirit of God: every spirit that acknowledges Jesus Christ come in the flesh belongs to God, and every spirit that does not acknowledge Jesus does not belong to God. This is the spirit of the antichrist that, as you heard, is to come, but in fact is already in the world. You belong to God, children, and you have conquered them, for the one who is in you is greater than the one who is in the world. They belong to the world; accordingly, their teaching belongs to the world, and the world listens to them. We belong to God, and anyone who knows God listens to us, while anyone who does not belong to God refuses to hear us. This is how we know the spirit of truth and the spirit of error and deceit.

Beloved, let us love one another, because love is of God; everyone who loves is begotten by God and knows God. Whoever is without love does not know God, for God is love. In this way the love of God was revealed to us: God sent His only Son into the world so that we might have life through Him. In this is love: not that we have loved God, but that he loved us and sent His Son as expiation for our sins. Beloved, if God so loved us, we also must love one another. No one has ever seen God. Yet, if we love one another, God remains in us, and His love is brought to perfection in us. This is how we know that we remain in Him and He in us, that he has given us of His Spirit. Moreover, we have seen and testify that the Father sent His Son as Savior of the world. Whoever acknowledges that Jesus is the Son of God, God remains in him and he in God. We have come to know and to believe in the love God has for us.

God is love, and whoever remains in love remains in God and God in him. In this is love brought to perfection among us, that we have confidence on the Day of Judgment because as He is, so are we in this world. There is no fear in love, but perfect love drives out fear because fear has to do with punishment, and so one who fears is not yet perfect in love. We love because he first loved us. If anyone says, "I love God," but hates his brother, he is a liar; for whoever does not love a brother whom he has seen cannot love God whom he has not seen. This is the commandment we have from Him: whoever loves God must also love his brother. (1John 1-2-3-4)

God loves you!

THE WHOLE DUTY OF MAN

I n conclusion, you must understand that everything and every evil and suffering in this world is not going to get any better. Wherever you want to write it, you can write it in the palm of your hands, you can write on the wall, or you can even write it on your Bible, but the main place you need to write it is in your mind, that the conditions of this world will not get any better. The only hope for the nations of the earth and the only hope for our world is the coming of the Lord Jesus Christ, the savior of the world. Things will not get better, you're going to have to get a real hold to Jesus and become just as fanatical about Jesus as you are about your inner idol.

Now, the last word, when all is heard: Fear God and keep His commandments, for this is man's all; because God will bring to judgement every work, with all its hidden qualities, whether good or bad.

Amen!

LETTER TO THE CHILDREN
OF ABRAHAM

My heart is inditing a good matter: I speak of the things which I have made touching the king: My tongue is the pen of a ready scribe.

Prophet Joseph, a scribe of Jesus Christ, called by the will of God according to the promise of the life that is in Christ.

To the children of Abraham, who are elect in the dispersion, called according to the foreknowledge of God the Father, in the sanctification of the Spirit, for obedience to Jesus Christ and for sprinkling with His blood.

To the Muslims, twelve princes, descendants of Ishmael: *(Nabaioth, Kedar, Adbeel, Mibsam, Mishma, Dumah, Massa, Hadad, Tema, Jetur, Naphish and Kedemah)*,

To the Jews, twelve tribes of Israel: *(Reuben, Simeon, Levi, Judah, Dan, Naphtali, Gad, Asher, Issachar, Zebulun, Joseph and Benjamin)*,

To the Descendants of Esau: *(Eliphaz, Reuel, Jeush, Jalam and Korah)*,

To the Sons of Keturah, Abraham's concubine: *(Zimran, Jakshan, Medan, Midian, Ishbak and Shuah)*,

To the Jews converted in Christ, from the twelve Apostles who announced to you the good news by the Holy Spirit: *(St. Peter, St. James, St. John, St. Andrew, St. Philip, St. Thomas, St. Bartholomew, St. Matthew, St. James son of Alphaeus, St. Simon the Zealot, St. Judas son of James and St. Matthias)*,

To the Gentiles Believers in Christ, from St. Paul the Apostle of Jesus Christ, who announced to you the Gospel of Christ,

And finally, to the World, those elected from before the foundation of the world and will obtain a faith in Christ of equal standing with ours,

May grace mercy and peace be multiplied to you in the knowledge of God and the Lord Jesus Christ, who gave himself for our sins to deliver us from the present evil age, according to the will of our God and Father, to whom be the glory forever and ever. Amen

First I thank my God through Jesus Christ for the grace given me to impart you some spiritual gift, for I long to see you. I want you to know, brothers, that I often intended to come to you (but thus far have been prevented), in order that I may reap some harvest among you as well as among the rest of the people. I am under obligation both to Muslims and to Jews, both to the Believers and to Christians, both to Gentiles and to Barbarians. So I am eager to preach the gospel of Christ to you also who are in the dispersion. For I am not ashamed of the gospel of Jesus Christ, for it is the power of God for salvation to everyone who believes, to the Muslims, to the Jews and to the Gentiles. For in it the righteousness of God is revealed from faith for faith.

Men, brethren, hearken, I now write unto you my first letter in which I am stirring up your sincere minds by way of remembrance, that you may be mindful of the words which were spoken before the holy prophets, that the God of glory appeared unto our father Abraham, when he was in Mesopotamia, before he dwells in Haran, and said unto him, Go out from your land, and from your kindred, and come into the land in which I will show you. Then came he out of the land of Chaldeans, and dwelt in Haran: and from thence, when his father was dead, he removed him into the land of Canaan (Israel), and he gave him none inheritance in it, no, not so much as to set his foot on; yet he promised that he would give it to him for a possession, and to his seed after him, when as yet he had no child. And God spake on this wise, that his seed should sojourn in a strange land; and that they should bring them into bondage, and entreat them evil for four hundred years. And the nation to whom they shall be in bondage will I judge, said God: and after that shall they come forth, and serve him. And he gave him the Covenant of Circumcision: and so Abraham begat Ishmael the father of the Muslims Nation, Abraham was ninety-nine years old when he was circumcised in the flesh of his foreskin. And Ishmael his firstborn son was thirteen years old when he was circumcised in the flesh of his foreskin. That very day Abraham and Ishmael were circumcised. But when the fullness of time had come, Abraham begat Isaac, son of the promise and circumcised him the eighth day.

Now, tell me, you that desire to be under the law, do you not hear the law? For it is written, that Abraham had two sons, the one by a bondmaid, a slave woman, the other by a freewoman. But he who was of the bondwoman was born after the flesh; but of the freewoman was born after the promise of God. Now this may be interpreted allegorically: for these are the TWO COVENANTS. The one from the Mount Sinai, which gendereth to bondage, bearing children for slavery, she is Agar. For this Agar is Mount Sinai in Arabia, she corresponds to the present Jerusalem, for she is in slavery with her children, namely the Muslims. But Jerusalem which is above is free, and she is the mother of all of us, she is Sarah. For it is written, Rejoice O barren that bearest not; break forth and cry aloud, you who are not in labor! For the children of the desolate one will be more than those of the one who has a husband. Now we, brethren, as Isaac was, are the children of the promise. But as then he that was born after the flesh persecuted him that was born after the Spirit, even so it is now. Nevertheless what does the Scripture says? Cast out the bondwoman and her son: for the son of the bondwoman shall not be heir with the son of the freewoman. So then, brethren, we are not children of the bondwoman, but of the free. I say the truth in Christ; I lie not, my conscience also bearing me witness in the Holy Spirit, that I have great heaviness and continual sorrow in my heart. For I could wish that myself were accursed from Christ for my brethren, who are Israelites; to whom belong the adoption, and the glory, and the covenants, and the giving of the law, and the service of God, and the promises; whose are the fathers, and of whom as concerning the flesh Christ came, who is over all, God blessed forever. Amen.

Not as though the Word of God has failed, nor has taken none effect. For not all who are descended from Israel belong to Israel, and not all are children of Abraham because they are his offspring, but through Isaac shall your offspring be called. This means that it is not the children of the flesh who are the children of God, but the children of the promise are counted as offspring. For this is the word of promise, at this time will I come, and Sarah shall have a son. And not only this; but when Rebecca also had conceived by one, even by our father Isaac; (for the children being not yet born, neither having done any good or evil, that the purpose of God according to election might stand, not of works, but because of his call. It was said unto her, the elder shall serve the younger. As it is written, Jacob have I loved, but Esau have I hated. What shall we say then? Is there unrighteousness with God? God forbid. For he says to Moses, I will have mercy on whom I will have mercy, and I will have compassion on whom I will have compassion. So then it depends not on human will or exertion, but on God, who has mercy. For the Scripture says to Pharaoh, For this very purpose I have raised you up, that I may show my power in you, and that my name might be declared throughout all the earth. Therefore he has mercy on whomever he wills, and he hardens whomever he wills. You will say to me then, why does he still find fault? For who can resist his will? But who are you, O man, to answer back to God? Will what is molded say to its molder, "Why have you make me like this?" Has the potter no right over the clay, to make out of the same lump one vessel of honored use and another for dishonorable use? What if God, desiring to show his wrath and to make known his power, has endured with much longsuffering the vessels of wrath fitted to destruction, in order to make known the riches of his glory on the vessels of mercy, which he has prepared before hand for glory. Even us whom he has called, not from the Jews only but also from the Gentiles? As indeed he says in Hosea, "Those who were not my people I will call my people, and her who was not beloved I will call beloved. And in shall come to pass, that in the place where it was said unto them, You are not my people; there shall they be called the children of God. And Isaiah cries out concerning Israel: Though the number of the children of Israel be as the sand of the sea, a remnant shall be saved. For the Lord will carry out his sentence upon the earth fully and without delay.

What shall we say then? That the Gentiles, which followed not after righteousness, have attained to righteousness, even the righteousness that is of faith. But Israel, which followed after the law of righteousness, has not attained to the law of righteousness. Wherefore? Because they sought it not by faith, but as it were by the works of the law. For they stumbled at that stumbling stone; As it is written, Behold, I lay in Sion a stumbling stone and rock of offence: and whosoever believe on him shall not be ashamed.

Brethren, my heart's desire and prayer to God for Muslims, Jews and Gentiles is, that they might be saved. For I bear them record that they have a zeal of God, but not according to knowledge. For they being ignorant of God's righteousness, and going about to establish their own righteousness, have not submitted themselves unto the righteousness of God.

For Jesus Christ is the end of the law for righteousness to everyone who believe.

"Oh, the depth of the richies both of the wisdom and knowledge of God! How unsearchable are his judgments, and his ways past finding out! For who has known the mind of the Lord, or who has been his counselor? Or who has first given to him a gift, that he might be repaid?" For of him, and through him, and to him, are all things: to whom be glory for ever. What then, have I then become your enemy by telling you the truth? They make much of you, but for no good purpose. They want to shut you out, that you may make much of them. Now Isaac, the son of the promise begat Jacob, whose name was changed to Israel; and Jacob begat the twelve patriarchs. And the patriarchs, moved with envy, sold Joseph into Egypt: but God was with him, and delivered him out of all his afflictions, and gave him favor and wisdom in the sight of Pharaoh king of Egypt; and he made him governor over Egypt and all his house. Now there came a famine throughout all the land of Egypt and Chanaan, and great affliction: and our fathers found no sustenance. But when Jacob heard that there was corn in Egypt, he sent out our fathers first. And at the second time Joseph was made known to his brethren; and Joseph kindred was made known unto Pharaoh. Then sent Joseph, and called his father Jacob to him, and all his kindred, threescore and fifteen souls (seventy-five persons). So Jacob went down into Egypt, and died, he, and our fathers, and were carried over in Sychem, and laid in the sepulchre that Abraham bought for a sum of money of the sons of Emmor the father of Sychem. But when the time of the promise drew nigh, which God had sworn to Abraham, the people grew and multiplied in Egypt, till another king arose, which knew not Joseph. The same dealt subtily with our kindred, and evil entreated our fathers, so that they cast out their young children, to the end they might not live. In which time Moses was born, and was exceeding fair, and nourished up in his father's house three months. And when he was cast out, Pharaoh's daughter took him up, and nourished him for her own son. And Moses was learned in all the wisdom of the Egyptians, and was mighty in words and in deeds. And when he was full forty years old, it came into his heart to visit his brethren the children of Israel. And seeing one of them suffer wrong, he defended him, and avenged him that was oppressed, and smote the Egyptian: for he supposed his brethren would have understood how that God by his hand would deliver them: but they understood not.

And the next day he appeared to them as they strove and tried to reconcile them, saying, Sirs, you are brethren; why do you wrong one another? But he that did his neighbor wrong thrust him away, saying, who made you a ruler and a judge over us? Do you want to kill me as you killed the Egyptians yesterday? Then fled Moses at this saying, and was a stranger in the land of Midian, where he begat two sons. And when forty years were expired, there appeared to him in the wilderness of Mount Sinai an angel of the Lord in a flame of fire in a bush. When Moses saw it, he wondered at the sight; and as he drew near to beholds it, the voice of the Lord came unto him, saying, I am the God of your fathers, the GOD OF ABRAHAM, AND THE GOD OF ISAAC, AND THE GOD OF JACOB. Then Moses trembled, and durst not behold. Then said the Lord to him, Put off your shoes from your feet: for the place where you are standing is holy ground. I have seen, I have seen the affliction of my people which is in Egypt, and I have heard their groaning, and am come down to deliver them. And now come, I will send you into Egypt. This Moses whom they refused, saying, who made you a ruler and a judge? The same did God send to be a ruler and a deliverer by the hand of the angel which appeared to him in the bush. He brought them out, after that he had performing wonders and signs in the land of Egypt, and in the Red sea, and in the wilderness forty years. This is that Moses, which said unto the children of Israel, A Prophet shall the Lord your God raise up unto you of your brethren, like unto me; him shall you listen. This is he, that was in the church in the wilderness with the angel which spoke to him in the Mount Sinai, and with our fathers: who received the lively oracles to give unto us: to whom our fathers would not obey, but thrust him from them, and in their hearts turned back again into Egypt, saying unto Aaron, (Moses' old brother) make us gods to go before us: for as for this Moses, which brought us out of the land of Egypt, we do not know what has become of him. And they made a calf in those days, and offered sacrifice unto the idol, and rejoiced in the works of their own hands. Then God turned, and gave them up to worship the host of heaven; as it is written in the book of the prophets, O, ye house of Israel, have you offered to me slain beats and sacrifices by the space of forty years in the wilderness? Yea, you took up the tabernacle of Moloch, and the star of your god remphan, figures which you made to worship them: and I will carry you away beyond Babylon. Our fathers had the tabernacle of witness in the wilderness, as he had appointed, speaking unto Moses, that he should make it according to the fashion that he had seen. Which also our fathers that came after brought in with JESUS into the possession of the Gentiles, whom God drave out before the face of our fathers, unto the days of David; who found favor before God, and desired to find a tabernacle for the God of Jacob. But Solomon built him an house. Howbeit the Most High does not dwell in houses made by hands, as the prophets say, Heaven is my Throne, and Earth is my footstool: what kind of house will you build for me, says the Lord, or what is the place for my rest? Did not my hands made all these things? You stiffnecked and uncircumcised in heart and ears, you do always resist the Holy Ghost; as your fathers did, so do you. Which of the prophets have not your fathers persecuted? And they have slain them which announced beforehand the coming of Jesus Christ, whom was betrayed and murdered. You who have received the law by the disposition of angels, and have not kept it. Be it known unto you all, and to all human races, that by the NAME OF JESUS CHRIST OF NAZARETH, who was crucified, which God raised from the dead, everyone who call on his name will be saved. But how are they to call on him whom they have not believed? And how are they to believe in him of whom they have never heard? And how are they to hear without someone preaching? And how are they to preach unless they are sent? As it is written, "How beautiful are the feet of them that preach the gospel of peace, and bring glad tidings of good things!" But they have not all obeyed the gospel. For Isaiah says, "Lord who has believed our report? So then faith comes by hearing, and hearing by the word of God. But I say, have they not heard? Yes verily, their sound went into all the earth, and their words unto the ends of the world. This Jesus is the stone which was set at nought of you builders, which is become the head of the corner. Neither is there salvation in any other: for there is none other name under heaven given among men, whereby we must be saved.

Brethren, hearken to these words, Jesus of Nazareth, a man approved by God by miracles and wonders and signs, which God did by him, Him being delivered by the determinate counsel and foreknowledge of God was crucified and slain by wicked hands. God raised him up, having loosed the pains of death: because it was impossible that he should be holden of it. For David says concerning him, I foresaw the Lord always before my face, for he is on my right hand, that I should not be moved: Therefore did my heart rejoice, and my tongue was glad; moreover also my flesh shall rest in hope: because you will not abandon my soul in hell, neither let your Holy One to see corruption.

Men and brethren, let me freely speak unto you of the patriarch David, that he is both dead and buried, and his sepulchre is with us unto this day. Therefore being a prophet, and knowing that God had sworn with an oath to him, that of the fruit of his loins, according to the flesh, he would raise up Christ to sit on his throne; He seeing this before spake of the resurrection of Christ, that his soul was not left in hell, neither his flesh did see corruption. This Jesus God raised up, and of that we all are witnesses. Being therefore exalted at the right hand of God, and having received from the Father the promise of the Holy Spirit, to be a Prince and a Savior, to give repentance, and forgiveness of sins to Israel, and to the world. And we are his witnesses of these things; and so is also the Holy Spirit, whom God has given to them who obey him.

Repent ye therefore, be converted, and be baptized every one of you in the name of Jesus Christ of Nazareth of Galilee, that your sins may be blotted out, that times of refreshing may come from the presence of the Lord and you shall receive the gift of the Holy Spirit. For the promise is unto you, and to your children, and to all that are afar off, even as many as the Lord our God shall calls to himself.

Amen

THE GREAT COMMISSION

And Jesus came and spake unto them, saying,

All power is given unto me in heaven and on earth. Go ye therefore *(St Matthew 28:18-19)* into all the world and preach the gospel to every creature *(St Luke 16:15).* Teach all nations, baptizing them in the Name of the Father, and the Son, and the Holy Ghost: Teaching them to observe all things whatsoever I have commanded you *(St Matthew 28:19-20).* He that believeth and is baptized shall be saved; but he that believeth not shall be damned.

And these signs shall follow them that believe; in my name shall they cast out devils; they shall speak with new tongues; they shall take up serpents; and if they drink any deadly thing, it shall not hurt them; they shall lay hands on the sick; and they shall recover *(St Mark 16:16-18).* And, Lo, I am with you always, even unto the end of the world.

Amen
(St Matthew 28:20)

KNOWING JESUS PERSONALLY

The Lord Christ is alive. Today He wants to come into your life, forgive your sins, and give you the power to live an abundant life. Read to His words, He says: "Come unto 'Me,' all you that labor and are heavy laden, and I will give you rest." "I AM the Way, and the Truth, and the Life, no man comes to the Father, except by Me." It is written, for all have sinned, and come short of the glory of God. It also written, for the wages of sin is death but the gift of God is Eternal Life through Jesus Christ our Lord. When Jesus died, He paid the penalty for your sins. Right now He is ready to come into your life. To experience His love and forgiveness and receive Eternal Life, you must accept as God's sacrifice for your sin and invite him to come into your life by faith. If this is the desire of your heart, you can pray a prayer of faith, and Jesus Christ will come in to your life. This is a suggest prayer,

"Lord Jesus, I need you, Forgive my sins, I believe and confess that you are the Lord, the Son of the Living God, and I also believe that God raised you from the dead. I thank you for coming and die on the cross for my sins, and redeemed me with your precious blood, to reconcile me with your Father. I open my heart and receive you as my Lord and Savior. I come to you with my heavy laden burden and I ask you to give me rest. I give you my heart, and my soul, and my spirit to make me the person that you called me to be, and that your will be done in my life. In your name Jesus I pray. "Amen."

If this prayer expresses the desires of your heart, then pray this prayer right now, where you are. Now that you have this prayer of faith and invited Jesus to come into your life, you can be sure that he came in because Jesus promised he would come in if only you would ask Him. You can also be sure that your sins are forgiven, that you are receive the power to become a child of God, and have eternal life. If you want to experience the full and abundant life which Jesus promised, talk with him in everyday at anytime in prayer. Discover his wonderful plan for your life by reading the Bible, and meet with other people who love and follow him.

Finally, remember always his wonderful promises: "I will never leave you nor forsake you. I am with you always, even to the end of the world.

SCRIPTURE REFERENCES

This book is breathed out by the Holy Spirit.
The original Scriptures are from the King James Version
TO GOD BE THE GLORY FOREVERMORE
Even so Amen!

CPSIA information can be obtained
at www.ICGtesting.com
Printed in the USA
BVHW032351220420
578018BV00019B/187